© 2021 Sharon Rush – Growise Publishing

Gastric Bypass Cookbook: Overcome Food Addiction & Avoid Regaining Weight After Bypass Surgery with 300 Delicious, Healthy & Easy Recipes. Take Care of Your New Stomach an 8 -Week Meal Plan

ISBN 9798481270227

01 02 03 04 05 06 07 08 09 10

All rights reserved.

Gastric Bypass Cookbook

Overcome Food Addiction & Avoid Regaining Weight After Bypass Surgery with 300 Delicious, Healthy & Easy Recipes. Take Care of Your New Stomach an 8-Week Meal Plan

Sharon Rush

© Copyright 2021 by Sharon Rush - All rights reserved.

This document is geared towards providing exact and reliable information in regards to the topic and issue covered. The publication is sold with the idea that the publisher is not required to render accounting, officially permitted, or otherwise, qualified services. If advice is necessary, legal or professional, a practiced individual in the profession should be ordered.

- From a Declaration of Principles which was accepted and approved equally by a Committee of the American Bar Association and a Committee of Publishers and Associations.

In no way is it legal to reproduce, duplicate, or transmit any part of this document in either electronic means or in printed format. Recording of this publication is strictly prohibited and any storage of this document is not allowed unless with written permission from the publisher. All rights reserved.

The information provided herein is stated to be truthful and consistent, in that any liability, in terms of inattention or otherwise, by any usage or abuse of any policies, processes, or directions contained within is the solitary and utter responsibility of the recipient reader. Under no circumstances will any legal responsibility or blame be held against the publisher for any reparation, damages, or monetary loss due to the information herein, either directly or indirectly.

Respective authors own all copyrights not held by the publisher.

The information herein is offered for informational purposes solely, and is universal as so. The presentation of the information is without contract or any type of guarantee assurance.

The trademarks that are used are without any consent, and the publication of the trademark is without permission or backing by the trademark owner. All trademarks and brands within this book are for clarifying purposes only and are the owned by the owners themselves, not affiliated with this document.

Table Of Content

Introduction 10

Chapter 1: Gastric Bypass Surgery 13
- 1.1 Roux-en-Y Gastric Bypass (RYGB) 13
  - 1.1.1 The Procedure 14
  - 1.1.2 How it Works? 14
  - 1.1.3 Is Gastric Bypass Right For You? 14
- 1.2 Assessment Before Surgery 16
- 1.3 What can you expect? 17
- 1.4 During the Procedure 17

Chapter 2: Risks & Solutions of the Stomach Bypass 19
- 2.1 Malnutrition 20
- 2.2 Leak in The Gut 20
- 2.3 Excess Skin 21
- 2.4 Clots in the Blood 21
- 2.5 Infection of the wound 21

Chapter 3: The Bariatric Diet & After Care 22
- 3.1 Fluids 22
- 3.2 Protein 22
- 3.3 Supplements 23
- 3.4 Foods to Avoid 23
- 3.5 Pre-operation Diet 24
- 3.6 Post Op-Diet & Stages 24
- 3.7. 5-Day Pouch Reset 25
- 3.8 Exercise Post-Op 25

Chapter 4: Stage 1 Diet & Tips 27
- 4.1 Stage 1: Clear Liquids 27
  1. Fat-Free Chicken Broth 29
  2. Low-Fat Vegetable Broth 29
  3. Sugar-Free Jello 30
  4. Beef Bone Broth 30

Chapter 5: Stage 2- Full liquids/Pureed Foods Recipes & Tips 31
1. Pureed Classic Egg Salad 33
2. Root Vegetable Soup 33
3. Garlic & Vegetable Soup 33
4. Chicken Clear Soup 34
5. Egg Whites 34
6. Low Carb Green Smoothie 34
7. Mango Peach Smoothie 35
8. Protein Hot Tea 35
9. Pineapple Coconut Smoothie 35
10. Chocolate Protein Shake 35
11. Easy Egg Custard 36
12. Watermelon Strawberry Protein Smoothie . 36
13. Creamy Healthy Soup 36
14. Pumpkin Carrot Soup 36
15. Orange Lemonade Protein Smoothie 37
16. Creamy Carrot & Ginger Soup 37
17. Blueberry Lemonade Vitamin Smoothie 37
18. Strawberry Greek Yogurt Whip 37
19. Light Tomato Soup 38
20. Mexican Egg Puree 38
21. Chimichurri Chicken Puree 38
22. Turkey Tacos with Refried Beans 38
23. Chicken & Black Bean Mole Puree 39
24. Eggnog Protein Shake 39
25. Pumpkin Pie Protein Shake 39
26. Gingerbread Cookie Protein Shake 39
27. Lemon Garlic Pureed Salmon 40
28. Single Serve Baked Ricotta 40
29. Creamy Shrimp Scampi 40

30. Chocolate Peanut Butter Protein Shake 40
31. Low-Fat Refried Beans 41
32. Pumpkin Chicken Soup 41
33. Red Pepper Enchilada Bean 41
34. Green Protein Smoothie 41
35. White Bean Soup 42
36. Carrot Lemonade Smoothie 42
37. Sweet Potato Puree 42
38. Buffalo Ranch Chicken 42
39. Chili Puree 43
40. No Chew Cheeseburgers 43
41. Italian Chicken Puree 43
42. Ricotta & White Bean Puree 43
43. Ginger Garlic Tofu Puree 44
44. Moroccan Fish Puree 44
45. Sesame Tuna Salad Puree 44
46. Caribbean Pork Puree 44
47. Rosemary Chicken with Blue Cheese 45
48. Mediterranean Chicken Puree 45
49. Pureed Chicken Breast Salad 45
50. Chicken & Sweet Potato Puree 45
51. Banana, Tofu & Pear Puree 45
52. Cheesy Cauliflower Puree 46
53. Basic Oatmeal 46
54. Peppermint Shake 46
55. Lemon Crystal Shake 46
56. Orange Tea 46
57. Pureed Vegetable 47

Chapter 6: Stage 3: Semi-Solid/Soft foods 48
1. High Protein Deviled Egg & Bacon 49
2. Baked Ricotta Florentine 49
3. Spinach Soup With Lemon 49
4. Scrambled Eggs With Black Bean 49
5. Pork Taco Soup 50
6. Greek Yogurt Parfait 50
7. Banana Spinach Protein Smoothie 50
8. Creamsicle 51
9. Mocha Java 51
10. Berry Bomb 51
11. Berry Avocado Smoothie 51
12. Tuscan White Bean Soup 51
13. Chocolate Cherry Shake 52
14. Turkey Kale Meatballs 52
15. Buffalo Chicken Meatballs 52
16. Ricotta Scrambled Eggs 53
17. Zucchini Soup 53
18. Crockpot Curry Chicken 53
19. Baked Fish with Almond Chutney 53
20. Cranberry, Sage & Gruyere Turkey Meatballs
.... 54
21. Juicy Jelly/Jello Pots 54
22. Spinach & Feta Bake 54
23. Soft Crab Salad 55
24. Spicy Vegetarian Chili 55
25. Power Chicken Salad 55
26. Parmesan & Roasted Fauxtatoe 55
27. Taco Casserole 56
28. Skinny Meatloaf Muffins 56
29. Spicy Summer Beans & Sausage 56
30. Strawberry Oatmeal Bars 57
31. Pina Colada Protein Shake 57
32. Best High-Protein Soup 57
33. Breakfast Bowls 57
34. Pumpkin Spice Hot Chocolate 58
35. Chicken & Peanut Stew 58
36. Scotch Eggs 58
37. High Protein Egg Salad 58
38. Smoked Salmon Pate 59
39. Crustless Quiche 59
40. Peanut Butter Protein Bars 59
41. Swede Soup 59
42. Chili Lime Turkey Burgers 60

43. Shakshuka 60
44. Spanakopita Chicken Patties 60
45. Cranberry Chicken Salad 61
46. Spinach & Mushroom Egg Cups 61
47. Italian Meatloaf 61
48. Creamy Tuscan Shrimp 61
49. Cheesy Chicken & Broccoli Casserole 62
50. Cauliflower "Fried Rice" 62
51. Bacon & Vegetable Soup 62
52. Great Northern Beans and Sausage 63
53. Instant Pot Turkey Chili 63
54. Chicken Taco Chili 63
55. Turkey Meatloaf 63
56. Granola Bar 64
57. Cocoa Almond Protein Smoothie 64
58. Hashbrown Egg Casserole 64
59. Lemon Garlic Salmon Baked 65
60. Lentil, Haricot Bean & Chickpea Soup 65

Chapter 7: Stage 4: General Phase 66

Part 1: Appetizers, Snacks & Sides 68

1. Mozzarella sticks 68
2. Avocado Mango Mash 68
3. Protein Strawberry Cheesecake Cheeseball 68
4. Zucchini Artichoke Bites 69
5. Stuffed Mushrooms 69
6. Pumpkin Spice Chia Seed Pudding 69
7. Instant Chicken Gravy 69
8. Caprese Snack Bowl 69
9. Chicken Salad Cucumber Bites 70
10. Zucchini Chips 70
11. Mock Mashed Potatoes 70
12. Soft Pretzels 70
13. Angelic Chicken 71
14. Refried Pinto Bean Dip 71
15. Chocolate Peanut Butter Protein Balls ... 71
16. Roasted Chickpeas 71
17. Chicken-Crusted Southwestern Pizza Rolls. 72
18. Grilled Asparagus 72
19. Buffalo Chicken Dip 72
20. Veggie Stackers 72
21. Breakfast Cookies 73
22. Edamame Avocado Hummus 73
23. Oven-Roasted Carrots 73
24. Spinach Artichoke Dip 73
25. Bacon Cheeseburger Meatballs 74
26. Strawberry Lemon Popsicles 74
27. Cajun Cauliflower Rice 74
28. Crustless Quiche 75
29. 3 Ingredient Protein Bites 75
30. Pumpkin Cheesecake Pudding Parfaits 75
31. Healthy Cheeseburger Bites 75
32. 5 Minute Cauliflower Ricotta Bake 76
33. Crab Rangoon Dip 76
34. Smoked Salmon Dip 76
35. Cheesy Stuffed Acorn Squash 76
36. Egg Bites 77
37. Turkey Roll-Ups 77
38. Blueberry Mug Cake 77
39. French Carrot Medley 77
40. Smoked Salmon Appetizer 78
41. Low-Carb Shrimp Dip 78
42. Spicy Salmon Poppers 78
43. 10-Minute Tuna Rolls 78
44. Tuna Stuffed Avocado 79

Part 2: Meat & Poultry Recipes 80

1. Creamy Chicken Casserole 80
2. Chicken & Fennel en Papillote 80
3. Teriyaki Beef Skewers 80
4. Chipotle Chicken Fajita Bowls 81
5. Chili with Ground Beef 81
6. Southwestern Chicken Meatballs 81

7. Caprese Hasselback Chicken 82
8. Chicken Breast with Steamed Vegetables .. 82
9. Smoky Cabbage Rolls 82
10. Pork Street Tacos 82
11. Chicken Spinach & Tomato 83
12. Low Carb Breakfast Burritos 83
13. Sour Cream Chicken Enchiladas 83
14. Healthy Orange Chicken 84
15. Asian Chicken Lettuce Wraps 84
16. Chicken Crust Pizza 85
17. Parmesan Chicken Nuggets 85
18. Asian Pork Tenderloin 85
19. Stuffed Peppers 85
20. Chicken Japchae 86
21. Balsamic Roast Chicken 86
22. Chicken Sweet Potato Curry 87
23. Apple Baked Stuffed Pork Chops 87
24. White Chicken Chili Verde 87
25. Spanish Chicken and Bean Stew 87
26. Barbeque Chicken Pizza 88
27. Sesame Chicken 88
28. Lemon Rosemary Chicken 88
29. Sheet Pan Pork Tenderloin Dinner 89
30. Chicken Pie 89
31. Black Bean & Brown Rice Casserole 89
32. Chicken Enchilada Casserole 90
33. Stuffed Portobello Mushrooms 90
34. Cajun Stuffed Chicken 90
35. Pizza Casserole 90
36. Cheesy Chicken & Broccoli Bake 91
37. Southwest Chicken with Rice 91
38. Cheesy Crustless Quiche 92
39. Bacon Cheeseburger Casserole 92
40. Crockpot Butter Chicken 92
41. Pulled Barbeque Chicken 93
42. Creamy Tuscan Garlic Chicken 93
43. Garlicky Greek Chicken 93
44. Cilantro Lime Chicken Thighs 93
45. Curried Pork Tenderloin with Apple Cider .. 94
46. Goat Cheese & Spinach Stuffed Chicken Breast 94
47. Primavera Stuffed Chicken 94
48. Cajun Chicken and Veggies 95
49. Sweet & Sour Pork 95
50. Chicken Meatballs & Cauliflower Rice 95
51. Greek Lemon Chicken Skewers 95

Part 3: Soups & Salads 97
1. Chicken Taco Soup 97
2. Dill & Caper Egg Salad 97
3. Butternut Squash Soup 97
4. Good Luck Greens Soup 98
5. Black Bean & Lentil Soup 98
6. Black & White Bean Greek Salad 98
7. Golden Red & Orange Bell Pepper Soup 98
8. Garden Salmon Salad 99
9. Avocado Tuna Salad 99
10. Mushroom Soup 99
11. Ground Beef Veggie Stew 100
12. Broccoli Cheese Soup 100
13. Best Chili 100
14. Cauliflower Soup 100
15. Easy Pork Posole 101
16. Creamy Chicken Soup 101
17. Acorn Squash Soup 101
18. Red Pepper, Squash & Harissa Soup 102
19. Mexican Cabbage Roll Soup 102
20. Zuppa Toscana Soup 102
21. Rainbow Power Salad with Roasted Chickpeas 103
22. Carne Asada Steak Salad 103
23. Healthy Grilled Chicken Salad 103
24. Grilled Steak Salad 103

25. Buttermilk Chicken with Chopped Salad. 104
26. Herbed Shrimp with Tomato-Spinach Salad 104
27. Sauteed Brussel Sprout Salad 104
28. Chicken, Red Potato & Green Bean Salad 104
29. Club Salad with Pulled Chicken 105
30. Grilled Chicken & Wheat-Berry Salad 105
31. Balsamic Watermelon Chicken Salad 105

Part 4: Fish & Seafood Recipes **106**
Tuna Patties 106
2. Shrimp & Sausage Cajun Pasta 106
3. Mustard Crusted Salmon 106
4. Garlic Shrimp & Veggie Foil Packs 106
5. Tilapia Piccata 107
6. Easy Fish Tacos 107
7. Veggie Bowls With Smoked Salmon 107
8. Sheet Pan Baked Tilapia 107
9. BBQ Roasted Salmon 108
10. Broiled Tilapia Parmesan 108
11. Halibut with Cilantro, Lime & Garlic 108
12. Oven Fried Fish 109
13. Low Carb Baked Fish 109
14. Salmon With Green Beans 109
15. Baked Cod with Goat's Cheese & Thyme 109
16. Salmon Protein Bowl 109
17. Roasted Asian Salmon 110
18. Salmon with Tomatoes-Olive-Pistachio Tapenade 110
19. Soy & Butter Salmon Parcels 110
20. Salmon With Cucumber Noodles & Thyme 111
21. Baked Mayo-Parmesan Fish 111
22. Baked Parmesan Salmon 111
23. Seared Salmon With Hollandaise 111
24. Coconut Fish Curry 112
25. Dijon Baked Salmon 112
26. Salmon Patties With Sauce 112
27. Seared Scallops & Cauliflower Rice Risotto 112
28. Seafood Chowder 113
29. Cashew, Chilli & Lime-Crusted Fish 113
30. Tandoori Salmon 113
31. Asian Shrimp & Brussels Sprouts 113
32. Brazilian Fish Stew 114
33. Scrambled Eggs With Smoked Salmon 114
34. Crisp-Skin Fish 114
35. Wild Baked Salmon 115
36. Green Beans & Shrimp Sheet Pan Meal... 115
37. Fish Taco Bowls 115
38. Creamy Fish Casserole 115
39. Ginger & Soy Salmon 116
40. Halibut Ceviche 116
41. Baked Salmon With Pesto & Tomatoes 116
42. Tzatziki Avocado Salmon Rolls 116
43. Thai Fish Curry 117
44. Roast Salmon With Preserved Lemon 117
45. Fish Cakes With Lemon Avocado Sauce. 117
46. Baked Halibut 117
47. Roasted Spiced Cod With Brussels Sprouts 118
48. Foil Baked Chilean Sea Bass 118
49. Grilled Salmon With Avocado Topping.... 118
50. Garlic & Lemon Shrimp 119
51. Easy Roasted Salmon 119
52. Garlic Lemon Shrimp 119
53. Scallops with Snow Peas & Orange 119

Chapter 8: 8-Week Meal Plan **120**
Stage-1: Week 1 120
Week 2 122
Week 3 123
Stage 2: Week 4 125
Week 5 126

Week 6.. 127

Stage 3: Week 7 129

Week 8.. 130

Conclusion **132**

Introduction

Introduction

Your healthcare practitioner may suggest weight reduction surgery if you are significantly overweight and have had difficulty reducing weight. Bariatric surgery is another name for weight reduction surgery. It's a good method to lose weight and lower your chance of developing weight-related disorders. Cardiovascular disease, high blood pressure, arthritis, stroke, diabetes and, sleep apnea are among them.

Bariatric & metabolic surgery are terms used to describe weight reduction surgery. These words are used to describe the effect of these procedures on the weight and health of patients' metabolisms. Your doctor will make modifications to your stomach as well as small intestine during this surgery to alter the way your stomach absorbs & digest food.

The following are some of the ways that gastric bypass may help you lose weight:

- Your stomach will only be able to handle small amounts of food, thus leading to overall reduced calorie intake
- Gut hormones will change, making you feel fuller as well as suppressing your appetite.
- Reversal of metabolic syndrome caused by obesity

These procedures are extremely efficient in controlling diabetes, hypertension, sleep apnea, and high cholesterol, among many other illnesses, about obesity. These procedures may also help to avoid future health issues. Patients with obesity who opt to get therapy may expect a higher quality of life and long life due to the advantages.

Metabolic and bariatric procedures have been developed over many years and are among the most thoroughly researched therapies in contemporary medicine. They are done utilizing minimally invasive surgical methods and tiny openings (laparoscopic & robotic surgery). These advances enable patients to have a significantly better experience, less pain, fewer problems, reduced hospital stay, and quicker recovery times. These procedures are safe, with fewer complication rates than popular procedures, including hip replacement, gallbladder removal, or hysterectomy. With these kinds of surgeries, the total number of calories becomes low as well as nutrients and vitamins, and it is necessary to take prescribed vitamins and nutrients.

Blood clots, internal bleeding, and Infection can be possible complications of surgery. An anastomosis is another danger. A new link made between the intestines and stomach after surgery will not heal properly and can leak. One of the most severe consequences of gastric bypass surgery is the leakage of digestive fluids and partly digested food via an anastomosis. But, with a healthy diet, vitamins intake and, excessive you can reduce weight and take care of your stomach. The key is consistency and not giving up hope.

Chapter 1: Gastric Bypass Surgery

One of the most popular types of weight-loss surgery is gastric bypass. The tip of the stomach is converted into a tiny gastric pouch during this surgery. One end of the small intestine is pulled up and linked to the gastric pouch. This is a one-way anastomosis. The small intestine loop's opposite end is rejoined to the small intestine lower down. This is a different kind of cross-connection. Food is subsequently diverted to a section of the digestive system that is farther down. It goes around the tummy. Because food no longer passes through the stomach, the body absorbs fewer calories. After you eat, you will feel fuller considerably quicker.

If one has a BMI of 40<, or a BMI of 35< combined with severe weight-related health issues, their healthcare practitioner may recommend this procedure. If the BMI is more than 40, one is likely to be at least 100 lbs. overweight.

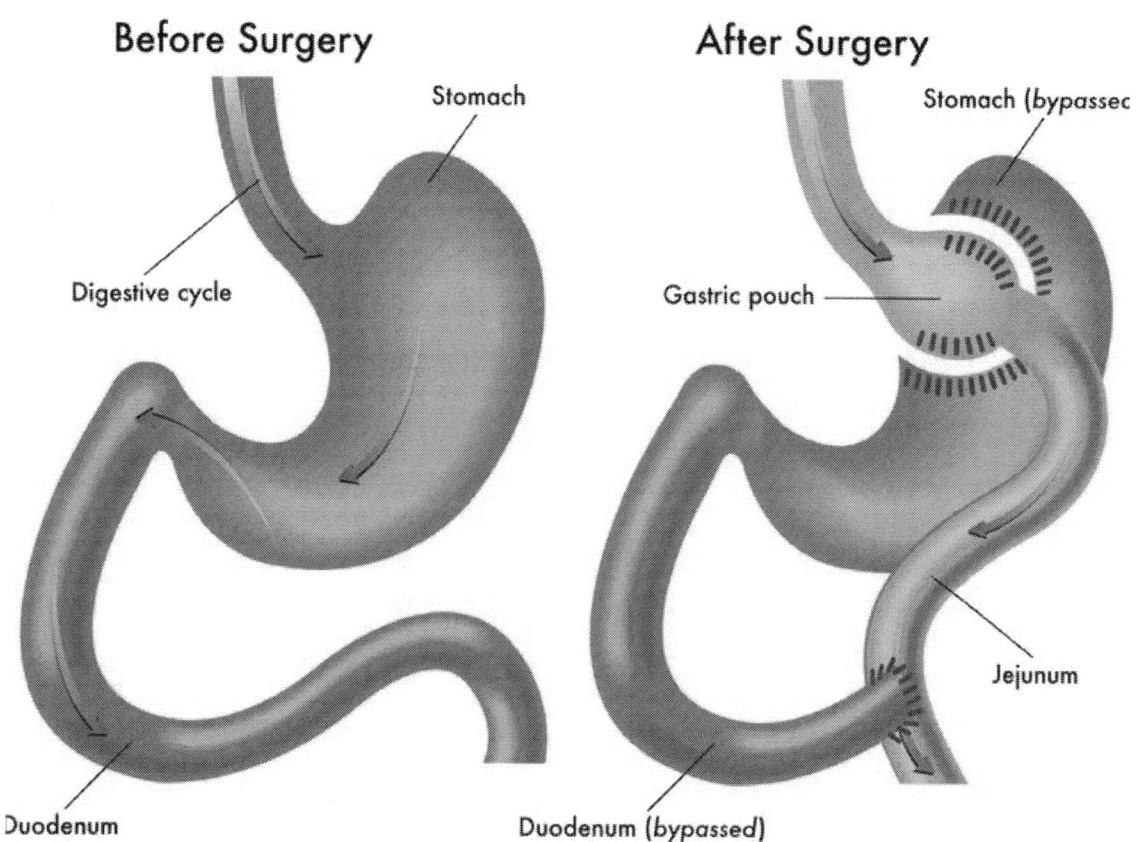

1.1 Roux-en-Y Gastric Bypass (RYGB)

The Roux-en-Y stomach Bypass, often known as the "gastric bypass," has been done for over fifty years, with the laparoscopic technique improved since 1993. It is one of the most frequent procedures for treating obesity and obesity-related illnesses, and it is highly successful. The name comes from a

French phrase that means "in the shape of a Y."

1.1.1 The Procedure

The stomach is separated into two sections: a tiny top section (pouch) approximately the size of an egg and a larger bottom portion (stomach). The stomach's bigger portion is skipped, and food is no longer stored or digested.

To enable food to pass, the small intestine is also separated and linked to the new stomach pouch. The small intestine segment that empties the bypassed or enlarged stomach is linked to the small intestine 3 to 4 feet downstream, producing a bowel connection that looks like a letter Y.

Food will eventually be mixed with stomach acids and digesting enzymes from the skipped stomach and early part of the small intestine.

- The doctor cuts 4-6 tiny incisions in your stomach during this procedure.
- These incisions are used to introduce the scope and equipment required to conduct the operation.
- In the surgery room, the camera is linked to a video display. This enables the surgeon to see into the stomach while doing the procedure.

Laparoscopy has several advantages to open surgery, including • A reduced hospital stay and a faster recovery

- Less discomfort
- Smaller scars and a decreased chance of infection or hernia

This procedure takes between 2 and 4 hours.

1.1.2 How Does It Work?

The gastric bypass procedure works in many ways. Like so many bariatric surgeries, the newly formed stomach pouch is smaller and can retain less food, consuming fewer calories. Furthermore, since the meal does not come into touch with the initial part of the small intestine, absorption is reduced. Most significantly, altering the food's path through the intestinal tract has a significant impact on appetite, satiety, and the body's ability to achieve and maintain weight reduction. Even before any weight reduction, the effect on hormones and metabolic health frequently leads to the recovery of adult-onset diabetes. Individuals with reflux (heartburn) benefit from the procedure, and their symptoms usually resolve rapidly. Individuals must avoid cigarette products and (NSAIDs) anti-inflammatory medications such as naproxen and ibuprofen, in addition to adopting proper dietary choices.

1.1.3 Is Gastric Bypass Right For You?

- Excellent short-term losing weight (60-80 % excess weight loss)
- Long-term, long-lasting results Most patients retain more than 50percent of their extra weight reduction up to 20 years following surgery, according to the study.
- Excellent results in the treatment of obesity-related health issues
- While this offers many advantages, it may also have the following drawbacks:
- The risk of complications is somewhat greater than with sleeve gastrectomy in the long run. However, complications may be prevented with careful management.

- After the operation, patients are not permitted to use aspirin or other NSAIDs.

All patients must take vitamins for the rest of their lives. If they wouldn't, long-term vitamin and mineral shortages, especially in vitamin B12, iron, folate, and calcium, may result in effective treatment of obesity-related diseases.

A technique that has been refined and standardized. The amount of weight you lose is determined by the kind of surgery one has and the changes you make in your lifestyle. Within 2 years, one may be able to shed up to 70% of your extra weight, if not more.

In addition to weight reduction, gastric bypass may help to alleviate or cure several diseases that are often associated with obesity, including as:

- Reflux disease
- Hypertension
- High cholesterol
- Obstructive sleep apnea (Osa)
- Infertility
- Heart disease
- Type 2 diabetes (T2dm)
- Stroke

Gastric bypass surgery may also enhance your capacity to do everyday tasks, thus improving your quality of life. When weight-loss surgery fails, there are other options.

It's likely to acquire weight following weight-loss surgery if you don't drop enough weight. If you don't make the suggested lifestyle adjustments, you may gain weight. If you regularly nibble on high-calorie meals, for example, your weight reduction may be insufficient. One must make lasting healthy dietary adjustments and engage in regular exercise to prevent regaining weight.

Following weight-loss surgery, it's critical to maintain all of your planned follow-up visits so that the doctor can track your progress. If you don't lose weight or have problems following your operation, contact your doctor right away.

Some disadvantages can happen, such as:

- It may be more difficult than a sleeve, a gastric band, or a gastrectomy.
- More micronutrient deficits than gastric banding or sleeve gastrectomy
- Small bowel blockage and consequences are a possibility.
- Ulcers are a possibility, particularly if you take NSAIDs or smoke.
- Can induce "dumping syndrome," a sensation of being ill after eating or drinking too much too fast especially sweets.

1.2 Assessment Before Surgery

Before having gastric bypass surgery, you'll be sent to a specialized clinic for an evaluation to see whether the procedure is right for you.

This may include looking at your:

- Physical health such as blood tests, scans, and X-rays are used to assess this.
- Eating habits and dietary patterns
- Mental health – this includes questions about your goals for surgery and if you have any mental health problems, all of which are used to determine whether you'll be able to handle the lengthy lifestyle adjustments required after surgery.

To assist decrease the size of the liver, you may be recommended to follow a calorie-controlled diet in the weeks leading up to surgery. This may help the surgery go more smoothly and safely.

Before Beginning the Procedure

Before you undergo this surgery, the surgeon will request testing and appointments with other health care professionals. Here are a few examples:

- A thorough physical examination.
- A gallbladder ultrasound
- Blood tests, and other testing to ensure you're healthy enough for surgery.
- Visits with the doctor to ensure that any other medical issues you may have been under control, like high blood pressure, heart & lung problems, or diabetes
- Nutritional guidance.
- Classes to help you understand what occurs during surgery, anticipate afterward, and what risks or complications may arise.

You should speak with a counselor to ensure that you are emotionally prepared for this procedure. After the operation, one must be able to make significant lifestyle adjustments.

If one smokes, they should quit a few weeks before surgery and not begin again after that. Smoking delays healing and raises the likelihood of complications. If you need assistance quitting, inform your doctor or nurse.

Inform the surgeon of the following:

- What medications, vitamins, other supplements, or herbs you're taking, even if you didn't get them from a doctor
- If you're pregnant or think you may be
- You may be advised to cease taking medications that make it difficult for the blood to clot during the week leading up to your operation. Ibuprofen, warfarin, and aspirin others are among them.
- Check with your doctor to see whether you should continue to take any medications on the day of the operation.
- Get the house ready for after the operation.
- Follow the directions for when to cease drinking and to eat on the day of operation.
- Take your medications with a tiny sip of water, as directed by your doctor.
- Be on time for your appointment at the hospital.

1.3 What can you expect?

This surgery is performed in a hospital setting. The hospital stay will usually last 1-2 days, but it may continue longer depending on your recovery.

Following the Surgery: most patients remain in the hospital for 1-4 days.

On the same day as the operation, you will be advised to sit on the edge of the room bed and move about a little bit.

- For one or two days, you may have a catheter inserted through the nose and into the stomach. This tube aids in the drainage of fluids from the gut.
- The bladder may also have a catheter in it to drain pee.
- For the first 1-3 days, you will be unable to eat. After that, liquids may be consumed, followed by pureed or soft meals.
- One may have a tube linked to the bypassed portion of the stomach. The catheter will be inserted into the side and used to remove the fluids.
- The legs will be fitted with specialized stockings to assist in preventing blood clots from developing.
- The medication will be given by injections to prevent blood clots.
- You'll be given pain medication. You'll either take pain medications or get pain medicine into your vein.

When you can consume liquid or pureed meals without vomiting and walk about without much discomfort, you will be allowed to return home.

Make sure you follow the directions for self-care at home. During the first year following surgery, most individuals lose approximately 10-20 pounds each month. The rate of weight reduction will slow down with time. You lose more weight if you stick to the food and activity plan from the start.

During the first 2 years, you may lose half or more of the excess weight. If you're still on a liquid or mashed diet following surgery, you'll lose weight rapidly.

Many medical problems may be improved by losing enough weight following surgery, including:

If you weigh less, it should be considerably simpler for you to walk about and perform your daily tasks.

One must follow their doctor's & dietitian's exercise and eating recommendations to reduce weight and prevent problems from the surgery.

1.4 During the Procedure

Before the operation, you will be administered a general anesthetic. During surgery, anesthesia is a medication that keeps you unconscious and pleasant.

The details of the gastric bypass are determined by your unique circumstances and the practices of the doctor. Some procedures need conventional big (open) abdominal incisions. The majority are done laparoscopically, which entails introducing tools into the belly via numerous tiny incisions.

After performing the incisions using an open or laparoscopic method, the doctor cuts across the top of the stomach, closing it off from the remainder of the stomach. The pouch that results is approximately the size of an egg and can only contain around 1 oz. of food. A stomach can usually contain approximately 3 quarts of food.

The surgeon next cuts the small intestine and sews a section of it into the pouch. Food then passes through this tiny pouch in the stomach and into the small intestine that is stitched to it. The majority of the stomach and the first portion of your small intestine is bypassed, and food enters the middle region of the small intestine straight.

Surgical procedures typically take a few hours. You will wake up in a recovery room after surgery, where medical personnel monitors you for any problems.

Chapter 2: Risks & Solutions of the Stomach Bypass

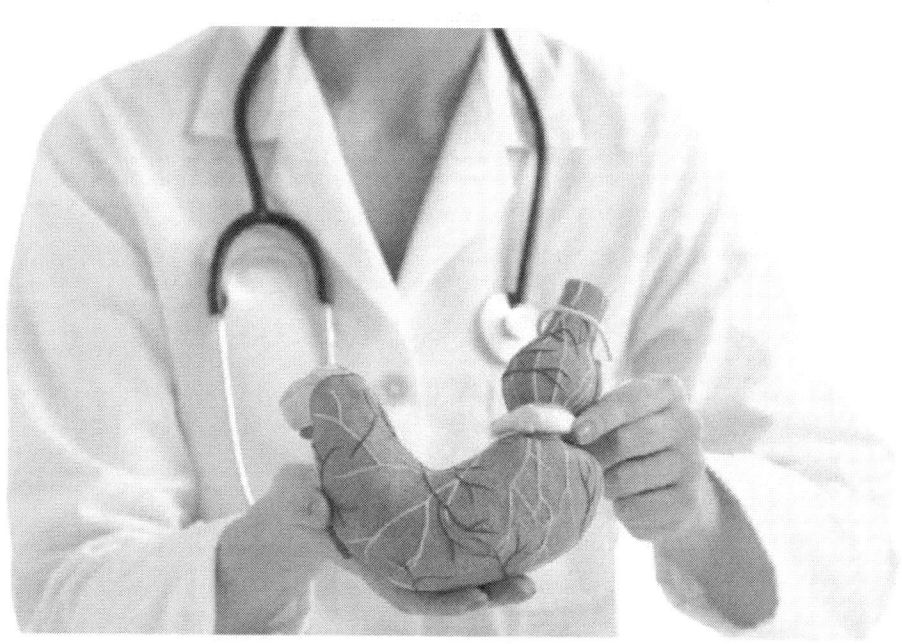

You would only be able to manage tiny quantities of soft food and drinks for the first month. However, after a while, you will slowly reintroduce solid meals into the diet. After about two teaspoons of food, you will realize that you are extremely full. Your doctor may also advise you to take nutritional supplements.

You may expect to lose half to 2/3rd of your extra body weight in the first 2 years. In most instances, weight reduction will continue for a year and a half before stabilizing.

Gastric bypass and other weight-loss procedures, like any major surgery, may have short- and long-term health consequences. The surgical technique has the same risks as any other abdominal surgery, including:

- Infection
- Adverse reactions to anesthesia
- Breathing problems
- Leaks in the gastrointestinal system
- Excessive bleeding
- Blood clots

- Expanding the pouch Over time, the stomach expands and stretches back to its former size.

- Lines of staples are broken down. The staples come undone.

- Deficiencies in vitamins, minerals, and nutrition. The body will have a harder time absorbing nutrients from meals.

- Stomal stenosis is a condition in which the stomach narrows. The link between the stomach and the small intestine narrows, producing vomiting, reflux, eventually an inability to eat, or nausea. It'll have to be dilated.

Dumping syndrome is another side effect. Food travels too rapidly from the stomach to the intestine when this occurs. After eating, side effects include weakness, sweating, nausea, fainting, and, on rare occasions, diarrhea, as well as being very weak.

Gallstones may form if one loses weight rapidly. If this occurs, the doctor may prescribe medication to dissolve them.

Because these procedures alter how your body processes food, you should see the doctor to ensure you receive all of the nutrients you need.

Longer-term risks can include:

- Hernias
- Stomach perforation
- Bowel obstruction
- Ulcers
- Gallstones
- Dumping syndrome, leading to vomiting, diarrhea, or nausea
- Low blood sugar (hypoglycemia)
- Vomiting
- Malnutrition

These complications can rarely be fatal.

2.1 Malnutrition

Weight reduction surgery may make it more difficult for the stomach to absorb minerals and vitamins from meals, putting you at risk of malnutrition.

The following symptoms may not always be obvious: • Constant Tiredness • Difficulty In Breathing • Heart Palpitations• Pale Complexion • Pins & Needles • Feeling Weak

Although a well-balanced diet may assist in minimizing the risk of malnutrition, most individuals will need additional nutritional supplements for the rest of their lives following surgery.

After the operation, you'll have frequent blood tests to check the mineral and vitamin levels so that any issues may be detected and addressed.

2.2 Leak in The Gut

There's a possibility that food may seep out into the gut in the days or even weeks after the surgery. This may result in a severe infection in the stomach.

A leak may cause the following symptoms: • A High Fever • Heart Palpation • Stomach Discomfort • Chills And Shivers • Rapid Breathing

If you experience any of these symptoms, contact your doctor as soon as possible. You may require surgery to fix the leak, as well as medicines to treat any infection.

2.3 Excess Skin

You may develop extra folds and skin rolls when you lose weight following surgery, especially around the breasts, stomach, hips, and extremities. Excess skin may be removed via surgery, such as a stomach tuck. However, since it is generally considered cosmetic surgery. Inquire with your doctor whether surgery to remove extra skin after weight reduction surgery is available

2.4 Clots in the Blood

After surgery, one will be given treatments to decrease the chance of blood clots, such as specialized leg stockings or blood-thinning drugs, but they may still happen.

Blood clots are most often seen in the lower leg or the lungs.

• The Lower Leg Becomes Uncomfortable, Achy, And Sensitive • Stiffness, Redness, Inflammation Or Warmth In The Lower Leg • A Sharp, Stabbing Chest Ache That Becomes Worse As You Breathe In • Difficulty Breathing Or A Cough • Getting Dizzy Or Fainting.

If you suspect you have a blood clot, call your doctor as soon as possible.

2.5 Infection of the wound

During the healing process, the wounds from the operation may get infected.

• Discomfort in or around the area • Red, Hot, And Swollen Skin • Liquid Flowing From The Wound Are All Signs Of Wound Infection.

If you suspect your wound is infected, see your doctor. A course of antibiotics may be prescribed.

These risks can be minimized if you follow your doctor's instructions, but sometimes these complications can occur. These conditions and their solutions should be discussed before the gastric bypass surgery with your doctor.

Chapter 3: The Bariatric Diet & After Care

Here are some general guidelines for the bariatric diet.
- Eat healthy, balanced meals in small amounts, and stick to a low-calorie, low-fat, and low-sugar diet.
- Keep track of the meal quantities and overall calorie and protein consumption regularly.
- Eat gradually and properly chew tiny pieces of food.
- Limit your intake of grains, bread, raw vegetables, and fresh produce, as well as tough-to-chew meats like steak. Meats that are ground are generally better accepted.
- Do not bite ice, use straws, or consume carbonated drinks. They may cause pain by introducing air into the pouch.
- Stay away from sugary meals and drinks, as well as strong sweets & fruit juices.
- The calorie consumption should be between 300-600 calories per day for the first 2 months after surgery, emphasizing light and clear or thick liquids.
- You should not consume more than 1,000 calories each day.

3.1 Fluids

- To prevent dehydration, drink lots of fluids and calorie-free fluids in between mealtime. Caffeine should be avoided in all beverages.
- Drink approximately 1 cup of liquids 6-8 times a day in between each light meal.
- At least 8 cups of fluids should be consumed each day. You'll be able to achieve this goal over time.

Do not consume any alcoholic drinks. Alcohol is absorbed considerably more rapidly into the system after surgery, making its narcotic and mood-altering effects more challenging to anticipate and manage.

3.2 Protein

Protein-rich meals help to preserve muscular tissue. Meats, fish, eggs, tuna, poultry, cottage cheese, soy milk, tofu, yogurt, and other milk products are all high in protein. A minimum of 65-75 g of protein per day should be the aim. Don't be concerned if you cannot achieve this objective during the first several months after surgery.

3.3 Supplements

To avoid nutritional inadequacies, one must take the prescribed supplements regularly. Remember to break or cut all tablets into 6-8 tiny pieces. You won't digest entire tablets as effectively as you did before surgery, and passing pills through the new anatomy may be challenging.

You'll start with a clear liquid diet right after the operation. After you've been released from the hospital, you may gradually reintroduce thicker liquids to your diet.

You can start eating blended and puréed meals two weeks after surgery. During this time, you may fulfill daily protein needs with liquid supplement beverages or powders that are rich in protein (> 20 g) and low in calories (< 200 calories).

It's essential to understand that the stomach will be extremely tiny after surgery. The hole via which food exits your stomach is likewise very small. As a result, while trying a new meal, just take 2-3 sips or nibbles at a time and wait ten minutes before trying again. This will assist you in determining your tolerance and limitations. Soft foods take longer to drain from the stomach than liquids.

You may feel nausea or discomfort if you overeat or quickly eat. Sauces, ice creams, and thick Gravies, examples of rich, creamy liquids to avoid initially.

Wait thirty minutes to drink anything after a meal and avoid drinking half an hour before a meal.

- Consume lean, protein-rich meals regularly.
- Choose low-fat and low-sugar meals and beverages.
- Stay away from alcoholic beverages.
- Avoid caffeine, which may dehydrate you.
- As recommended by your healthcare practitioner, take vitamin and mineral supplements regularly.
- Once you've progressed beyond liquids alone chew meals thoroughly until they're pureed before swallowing.

3.4 Foods to Avoid

Some beverages should be prohibited following bariatric surgery because they may irritate the recovering stomach:

- Carbonated & caffeinated drinks for at least three months after surgery •
- No alcoholic drinks for at least six months after operations
- Hard or dry red meat • Oily, high-fat meals
- Spicy or strongly seasoned meals
- Sugar alcohols including mannitol, erythritol, glycerol, sorbitol xylitol • Microwave-reheated foods

However, dumping is an unpleasant experience that you should avoid.

To minimize the danger of dumping, take the following steps:

- Limit your intake of high-sugar, refined-carbohydrate meals.
- Consume food slowly.
- Take your time chewing foods.

Certain meals are very hard to digest and should be avoided:

Pork, Grapes, Beef, Nuts, Whole Grains, Shellfish, Corn & Beans

3.5 Pre-operation Diet

The following items will be included in the 1 to 2-week pre-surgery diet:
- The diet's mainstay will be meal replacement drinks or protein shakes.
- Only non-sugar drinks are permitted (sugar substitutes are alright).
- There are no carbonated or caffeinated drinks allowed.
- Soup broth with no solids bits is OK to eat.
- Vegetable juice & V8 are also allowed.
- You may also consume a very light cream of wheat or cream of rice.

1-2 daily meals of lean meat with or without vegetables may be permissible, but only if the surgeon or certified dietician approves.

All liquids and drinks should be drunk gradually. Drinks should not be drunk with meals, and you should wait at least half an hour after or before eating.

Separating the liquids and solids is a great method to start before surgery.

3.6 Post Op-Diet & Stages

10 High-protein foods that one can eat after surgery
- Fish
- Skinless chicken
- Flakes
- Lean pork
- Lentils
- Eggs
- Beans
- Turkey
- Soya
- Yogurt
- Squash

After the operation, there are four stages.
- Stage 1 is based on clear liquids.
- Stage 2 is based on pureed meals & full liquids.
- Stage 3 is based on semi-solid meals or soft foods.
- Stage 4 is based on regular meals.

3.7. 5-Day Pouch Reset

Try the five-Day Pouch Reset to resume weight reduction after gastric bypass. If you feel like the surgery isn't pushing the cravings away like it used to. This is a high-protein, brief diet that may help you lose weight & reset your appetite level.

Only supplements are used in the 5-Day Pouch Reset regimen.

It is not advised to supplement your regular food 100 percent of the time; brief liquid and supplement diets may be extremely safe and beneficial. After you've "adjusted" your hunger level, you'll be able to switch to a whole diet and utilize protein supplements to help meet your daily protein need.

The 5-day pouch rest is good for when the weight loss has stopped

- You have gained some weight
- You haven't been monitoring daily food consumption
- You want to regain control over the eating, the Pouch Reset is for you.

Here's how the next five days will look

Liquid Supplements on Days One & Two

Only fluid protein supplements are used for the first two days. Protein soups and smoothies are good examples of this. Using the soups as the main meals and the delicious protein shakes as the "snacks" in-between meals.

3 to 5th Days: Supplements: Liquid plus Solid

The last three days are ideal for using solid protein supplements to make you feel satisfied for longer. It's also a good way to ease back into solid meals while still receiving 90 g of protein and limiting calories.

3.8 Exercise Post-Op

Physical exercise will aid in the recovery after weight reduction surgery. It will aid in improving circulation, prevention of blood clots helps in bowel function and wound healing. You may begin walking within the first week. At first, attempt to go for many short walks each day. At home, you may walk about, shower, and utilize the stairs. In 2-4 weeks after laparoscopic surgery, you should be able to resume most of the normal activities. If you undergo open surgery, it may require up to twelve weeks.

- Begin the fitness routine slowly and progressively increase the amount of time you spend exercising. Increase the number of repetitions, duration, or distance if it becomes too simple.
- Always remember that if anything hurts when you do it, then you should quit doing it.
- Set precise, attainable, and reasonable objectives for the fitness routine.
- Change up the exercises to avoid monotony.

- Pick a regular physical activity you love since you'll be more inclined to stick with them.
- Exercises that may be integrated into daily life, like gardening, cycling, brisk walking, may be simpler to stick to.
- Determine the ideal time to exercise; you may like to exercise early in the morning or late at night.
- Leave one's walking shoes or workout gear in the vehicle.
- Purchase a pedometer and set a goal of walking 10,000 steps each day.
- Always wait at least two hours after eating before beginning an exercise routine to prevent heartburn, knotting, or indigestion.
- After an exercise, let the muscles at least 24 hours rest so they can strengthen and heal correctly.

Stay hydrated by drinking lots of water. Because of the smaller stomach after surgery, it may be difficult for the body to process the water it needs, particularly during and after activity. Always have a bottle of water at the side and drink it on a routine basis.

Chapter 4: Stage 1 Diet & Tips

4.1 Stage 1: Clear Liquids

You will begin a clear liquid diet the day following the operation and continue for approximately 1 to 3 weeks. During this period, the patient should make every effort to drink 3 oz. of clear fluids every half an hour. This may be tough after the surgery, but it will get quicker and easier with time. Drink carefully at this time and avoid drinking liquids via a straw or chewing gum since these may cause gas and bloat. During this period, some drinks to try include:

- Apple juice, diluted
- Pedialyte Popsicles
- Lemon water
- Sugar-free citrus gelatin

Protein smoothies that have been diluted should also be included in the diet. Half protein shake + half water is a good combo. On the day of surgery, you'll be on a Phase One diet.

The first stage includes sugar-free clear liquids and Jell-O, as well as broths and water. No sugar, carbonated or caffeinated drinks should be eaten. These will have unpleasant side effects as well as the potential for problems. Make it a point to eat every 3 to 4 hours and avoid skipping any meals. Every meal should be around a half cup or 2 oz. in size. During this period, you should continue to consume at least 48 to 64 oz. of water.

- Stay hydrated by drinking lots of clear drinks. If you're having difficulty staying hydrated, ask the doctor about electrolytes beverages like Gatorade, which are low in calories.
- Nothing sweet should be consumed. Dumping syndrome is a problem that occurs when too much sugar enters the small intestine too fast. Intense nausea, tiredness, diarrhea, and even vomiting may occur as a consequence of this. Sugar also contains a lot of empty calories. This should be prevented for the time being and reduced in the long run.
- Caffeine may cause dehydration, acid reflux; therefore, it's best to avoid it. Carbonated drinks, such as those containing sugar, no-calorie alternatives, and seltzer, may all cause gas and bloating. All of these should be prevented afterward, if not permanently.

Choices Of Clear liquids

- Herbal tea, traditional & fruit tea-unsweetened
- Water
- No-sugar-added ice lollies, cordials, Jell-O & squashes
- Clear broths
- Decaffeinated coffee
- Whey protein drink (fruit) mix with water

1. Fat-Free Chicken Broth

Preparation time: 2 hours | Cooking time: 10 minutes | Serving: 1

Ingredients
- Black pepper, to taste
- Salt, to taste
- 1 Whole Chicken
- Garlic powder, to taste

Directions
1. In a pot, add all ingredients with enough water to completely cover the chicken.
2. Let it boil; keep skimming the bubbles on top.
3. Keep in the fridge for 2 hours, skim the fat off
4. Serve and save the rest for another use.

Nutrition Per serving: Kcal 327 | Sodium 106 mg | Protein 45 g | Carbs 6 g | Fat 105 g | Potassium: 101 mg

2. Low-Fat Vegetable Broth

Preparation time: 20 minutes | Cooking time: 20 minutes | Serving: 1

Ingredients
- Chopped carrots: 2.1 oz.
- Water: 6 cups
- Chopped green beans: 5.2 oz.
- Dried basil, thyme & sage: half tsp.
- Chopped celery: 4.2 oz.
- 4 cubes of low-sodium chicken stock

Directions
1. In a pot, add water and cubes, let it come to a boil.
2. Add the rest of the ingredients. Let it boil again and simmer for 15 minutes.
3. Strain and cool slightly, serve.
4. Save the rest for another use.

Nutrition Per serving: Kcal 217 | Sodium 121 mg | Protein 34 g | Carbs 5.3 g | Fat 67.2 g | Potassium: 76 mg

3. Sugar-Free Jello

Preparation time: 5 hours & 10 minutes | Cooking time: 20 minutes | Serving: 1

Ingredients
- Strawberries: ¼ cup
- Gelatin powder: half tbsp.
- Water: 2 cup
- No calorie sweetener: 3 tbsp.

Directions
1. In a pan, add strawberries and mix with water (half), let it come to a boil. Keep mashing them.
2. Simmer on low flame for 8 to 10 minutes.
3. In a bowl, add the rest of the water and mix with gelatin and let it rest for five minutes.
4. Pass the mashed strawberries throw a fine-mesh sieve, straining well. Add enough water to make it 3 cups.
5. In a pan, add strawberry juice and mix with a sugar substitute.
6. Cook on low for 2 minutes, add gelatin and cook until it dissolves.
7. Pour in a baking dish and keep in the fridge for 5-6 hours.
8. Slice and serve.

Nutrition Per serving: Kcal 232 | Sodium 11 mg | Protein 8 g | Carbs 1.3 g | Fat 1.4 g | Potassium: 12 mg

4. Beef Bone Broth

Preparation time: 10 minutes | Cooking time: 3-4 hours & 20 minutes | Serving: 1

Ingredients
- 1 carrot, chopped
- Whole peppercorns: ¼ tsp.
- Half of a bay leaves
- 1 celery stalk, chopped
- 1-2 sprigs of parsley
- Beef bones with marrow: 1 pound
- 1 smashed garlic clove
- Kosher salt, to taste
- Coldwater: 6 cups
- 1 sprig of fresh thyme
- Cider vinegar: 2 tbsp.

Directions
1. In a crockpot, add all ingredients.
2. Boil on high heat and simmer on low flame; keep skimming the fat on the surface.
3. Simmer until only 2 cups of liquid remains. Strain, cool slightly and serve.

Nutrition Per serving: Kcal 276 | Sodium 13.9 mg | Protein 21.9 g | Carbs 1.8 g | Fat 4.89 g | Potassium: 11.4 mg

Chapter 5: Stage 2- Full liquids/Pureed Foods Recipes & Tips

Consuming protein shakes should be maintained between meals, with a daily protein target of 80 to 100 g. Start with sugar-free almond or soy milk, but steer clear of cow's milk. In this stage, one should start adding supplements, one at a time.

Foods like skim milk, richer low-fat soups, and skim soy drinks are good examples of thicker liquids.

At the end of the day, you should be able to meet the protein needs without the need for supplements.

In stage 2, the same restrictions apply to stage 1: no caffeine, carbonated drinks, or sugar. New meals should be tried with caution; certain things you might stomach before the operation may not be tolerated afterward.

A Phase Two diet may help minimize staple line leaking by allowing the new pouch to recover. Patients who attempted to increase their diets too soon have experienced severe pain and nausea. Each meal should be around a half cup or 4 oz. in size, and these items should be simple to break apart with a fork. Even if this quantity hasn't been achieved, one should quit eating as soon as they are full.

- Greek or non-dairy yogurt are some examples of things you may consume at this period.
- Cream of wheat or Oatmeal
- Pureed banana
- Pea soup, cream of mushroom soup, etc.
- Lentils, fat-free refined beans, Black beans,

- Cheesy cottage with baby food
- No-sugar protein shakes
- Sugar-free applesauce
- Breakfast drinks
- Smooth, pureed broth & cream-based soups
- Unsweetened milk
- Nonfat pudding, Greek yogurt no-sugar-added
- Ice cream, sorbet, frozen yogurt, no-sugar-added
- Diluted smooth fruit juices

Tips for Stage 2
Here are some suggestions to help you stay healthy and happy when you're in the second stage:
- Gradually eat (or drink). Finish the food in approximately half an hour.
- Liquids that are at room temperature or slightly warm may be more tolerable.
- Keep track of the consumption using a cup with proportions and avoid straws.
- Use a baby spoon to eat slowly and set it down after a few bites.
- Mix in a little quantity of protein powder to boost the protein content of drinks. Powdered nonfat milk can also be used.
- To increase protein while minimizing fat and calories, make puddings, soups, and other dishes using nonfat milk.
- Use only protein powder with less than 3 g of fat, less than 12 g of carbohydrate, and at least 10 g of protein/ 100 calories.
- Make it a habit to maintain a food journal right now.
- Take the multivitamins and any additional vitamins suggested by the dietician or doctor.

1. Pureed Classic Egg Salad

Preparation time: 10 minutes | Cooking time: 0 minute | Serving: 1

Ingredients

- Salt & pepper to taste
- Mayonnaise: 1 tbsp., low-fat
- 1 soft-boiled egg
- Greek yogurt: 1 tbsp., low-fat

Directions

1. In a food processor, add all ingredients.
2. Pulse until smooth.

Nutrition Per serving: Kcal 176 | Sodium 144.9 mg | Protein 9.3 g | Carbs 4.6 g | Fat 13.2 g | Potassium: 12 mg

2. Root Vegetable Soup

Preparation time: 10 minutes | Cooking time: 40 minutes | Serving: 1

Ingredients

- 1 small sweet potato, peeled & cubed
- Water: 5 cups
- 1 leek, chopped
- 1 peeled parsnip, diced
- 1 chopped carrot
- Salt & pepper, to taste
- 1 turnip, peeled and diced
- Half onion, diced

Directions

1. In a large pan, add all ingredients.
2. Stir and let it come to a boil, simmer until all vegetables are tender.
3. Drain all but 1 cup of water.
4. Puree with an immersion blender, add more water to your desired consistency.
5. Serve.

Nutrition Per serving: Kcal 245 | Sodium 12.9 mg | Protein 18.2 g | Carbs 2.6 g | Fat 8.7 g | Potassium: 11.6 mg

3. Garlic & Vegetable Soup

Preparation time: 15 minutes | Cooking time: 35 minutes | Serving: 1

Ingredients

- 3 peeled carrots, diced
- Olive oil: 1 tsp.
- Salt & pepper to taste
- 2 sliced leeks
- Low-fat milk: 4 tbsp., unsweetened
- 6 chopped garlic
- Half head cauliflower, chopped
- 1 can of (14 oz.) Chopped tomatoes with liquid
- Half head of cabbage, chopped
- Tomato puree: 4 tsp.
- Water: 4 cups

Directions

1. In a pan, saute leeks, cabbage, cauliflower and carrot, cook until it wilts.
2. Add garlic, tomato puree and cook for 1-2 minutes.
3. Add 2 cups of water and simmer for ten minutes.
4. Add chopped tomatoes and the rest of the water and boil.
5. Turn the heat to low and cook for 20 minutes on low flame.

6. Puree with an immersion blender. Add milk and cook for 1 minute.
7. Serve with salt & pepper on top. Serve and save the rest of lunch or dinner.

Nutrition Per serving: Kcal 232| Sodium 11.9 mg | Protein 8.9 g | Carbs 2.81 g | Fat 7.3 g | Potassium: 9 mg

4. Chicken Clear Soup

Preparation time: 5 minutes| Cooking time: 25 minutes | Serving: 1

Ingredients

- 2 smashed garlic cloves
- Salt & pepper to taste
- Chopped carrot: 2 tbsp.
- Water: 2 1/2 cups
- Half bay leaf
- Bone-in chicken: 2.5 oz.
- 1-2 sprigs of thyme

Directions

1. In a pressure cooker, add all ingredients, stir and cook on high flame for 1 whistle.
2. Cook for 10 to 12 minutes on low flame.
3. Turn the heat off and release the pressure, strain the soup.
4. Shred the chicken, add it back to the pot.
5. Puree with an immersion blender. Serve.

Nutrition Per serving: Kcal 172| Sodium 71 mg | Protein 14 g | Carbs 2 g | Fat 11 g | Potassium: 190 mg

5. Egg Whites

Preparation time: 5 minutes| Cooking time: 10 minutes | Serving: 1

Ingredients

- 2 egg whites
- Salt & pepper, to taste

Directions

1. Boil a pot of water.
2. Swirl the water with a spoon, add the egg whites to a large spoon.
3. Carefully add to the water. Cook until they are no longer opaque, take out on a plate
4. Serve with salt & pepper.

Nutrition Per serving: Kcal 56| Sodium 5 mg | Protein 9 g | Carbs 1 g | Fat 1 g | Potassium: 0.2 mg

6. Low Carb Green Smoothie

Preparation time: 5 minutes| Cooking time: 10 minutes | Serving: 1

Ingredients

- Lemon juice: half tbsp.
- Half cup of spinach

- Peanut butter powder: half tbsp.
- Unsweetened coconut milk: 1/3 cup
- Half avocado
- Vanilla protein powder: half scoop, no-sugar-added

Directions

1. In a blender, add all ingredients.
2. Pulse until smooth.
3. Serve.

Nutrition Per serving: Kcal 101| Sodium 12 mg | Protein 19 g | Carbs 2 g | Fat 1.9 g | Potassium: 21 mg

7. Mango Peach Smoothie

Preparation time: 10 minutes | Cooking time: 0 minute | Serving: 1

Ingredients

- Greek-style yogurt: 1 cup, non-fat
- Frozen mango: half cup
- Skim milk: half cup
- Frozen peaches: half cup

Directions

1. In a blender, add all ingredients.
2. Pulse until smooth.
3. Serve.

Nutrition Per serving: Kcal 127| Sodium 11.9 mg | Protein 8 g | Carbs 6 g | Fat 4.9 g | Potassium: 27 mg

8. Protein Hot Tea

Preparation time: 10 minutes | Cooking time: 3 minutes | Serving: 1

Ingredients

- Protein water: 1 cup
- Peach perfect tea: 1 teabag

Directions

1. In a mug, add water and microwave until hot.
2. Add the tea bag, let it steep as per instructions, serve with 2-3 mint leaves in it.

Nutrition Per serving: Kcal 78| Sodium 1.9 mg | Protein 6 g | Carbs 0 g | Fat 0 g | Potassium: 0 mg

9. Pineapple Coconut Smoothie

Preparation time: 10 minutes | Cooking time: 0 minute | Serving: 1

Ingredients

- Shredded coconut: 1 tbsp.
- Skim milk: 2-4 tbsp.
- Frozen pineapple: 1 cup, chunks

- Greek yogurt: half cup, non-fat

Directions

1. In a blender, add all ingredients.
2. Pulse until smooth.
3. Serve.

Nutrition Per serving: Kcal 124| Sodium 13.2 mg | Protein 3.4 g | Carbs 4.8 g | Fat 12 g | Potassium: 35 mg

10. Chocolate Protein Shake

Preparation time: 10 minutes | Cooking time: 0 minute | Serving: 1

Ingredients

- Cocoa powder: 1 tbsp., unsweetened
- Chocolate flavor protein powder: 1 scoop
- Skim milk: 1 cup
- No-calorie sweetener, to taste
- Chocolate syrup: 2 tbsp., no-sugar-added

Directions

1. In a blender, add all ingredients.
2. Pulse until smooth.
3. Serve.

Nutrition Per serving: Kcal 145| Sodium 14.9 mg | Protein 15.8 g | Carbs 4 g | Fat 11.1 g | Potassium: 216 mg

11. Easy Egg Custard

Preparation time: 10 minutes | Cooking time: 20 minutes | Serving: 1

Ingredients

- Granulated sugar substitute: 1/4 cup
- Cornstarch: 1 tsp.
- Skim milk: ¾ cup
- Vanilla extract: 1/4 tsp.
- 1 egg yolk

Directions

1. In a pan, add sugar, extract and milk. Place on low flame, do not boil or simmer but make sure sugar dissolves.
2. Whisk well the egg yolks with cornstarch
3. Turn the flame off and add a few tablespoons of warm milk to the egg mixture. Mix well and pour half of the warm milk mixture while keep whisking. Add the rest and pour the mixture back into the pan.
4. Place on low flame, whisking until it thickens.
5. Serve warm.

Nutrition Per serving: Kcal 209 | Sodium 64 mg | Protein 6 g | Carbs 33 g | Fat 5.8 g | Potassium: 216 mg

12. Watermelon Strawberry Protein Smoothie

Preparation time: 10 minutes | Cooking time: 0 minute | Serving: 1

Ingredients

- watermelon Vitamin Powder: 1 scoop
- Skim Milk: 1 cup
- 1 to 2 Mint Leaves
- Watermelon Chunks: 1 cup
- 3 Strawberries
- Ice cubes, as needed

Directions

1. In a blender, add all ingredients.
2. Pulse until smooth.
3. Serve.

Nutrition Per serving: Kcal 121 | Sodium 21 mg | Protein 8 g | Carbs 4.1 g | Fat 12 g | Potassium: 106 mg

13. Creamy Healthy Soup

Preparation time: 10 minutes | Cooking time: 20 minute | Serving: 1

Ingredients

- Chicken broth: 2 cups, no-salt-added
- 0% fat milk: 1 cup
- 1 peeled zucchini, cut into slices
- 1 garlic clove
- Water: 2 cups
- Black pepper, to taste
- Garlic & onion powder: 1/4 tsp., each

Directions

1. In a pot, add all ingredients, do not add milk yet.
2. Let it simmer on a medium flame for 15 minutes, till zucchini is soft.
3. Turn the heat off and add milk, purree with a hand blender.
4. Add salt and pepper, serve.

Nutrition Per serving: Kcal 144 | Sodium 351 mg | Protein 14 g | Carbs 15 g | Fat 4 g | Potassium: 567 mg

14. Pumpkin Carrot Soup

Preparation time: 10 minutes | Cooking time: 30 minutes | Serving: 1

Ingredients

- Ground turmeric & curry powder: ¼ tsp.
- Chili flakes, to taste
- Peeled & cubed carrots: 1 cup
- Salt & pepper, to taste
- 1 sliced garlic clove
- Olive oil: 1 tsp.
- Coconut milk: 1/3 cup
- Peeled & cubed pumpkin: 1 cup
- Lemon juice: half tsp.
- Chicken broth: 1 ½ cups, low-salt

Directions

1. In a pot, saute garlic in oil for 1 minute. Add spices and cook for 1 minute.
2. Add vegetables and cook for few minutes.
3. Add the liquids, let it come to a boil.
4. Turn the heat low and simmer for 15 minutes till the vegetables are tender.
5. Turn the heat off, puree with a hand blender.
6. Adjust seasoning and serve.

Nutrition Per serving: Kcal 84 | Sodium 56 mg | Protein 3 g | Carbs 19 g | Fat 1 g | Potassium: 786 mg

15. Orange Lemonade Protein Smoothie

Preparation time: 10 minutes | **Cooking time:** 0 minute | **Serving:** 1

Ingredients

- 1 lemon's juice
- Water, as needed
- Orange juice: 6 oz.
- Spinach: 1 cup
- 5 to 6 ice cubes
- 1 frozen banana
- Lemonade Vitamin Powder: 1 scoop

Directions

1. In a blender, add all ingredients.
2. Pulse until smooth.
3. Serve.

Nutrition Per serving: Kcal 115 | Sodium 11.1 mg | Protein 8 g | Carbs 3.2 g | Fat 8.4 g | Potassium: 116 mg

16. Creamy Carrot & Ginger Soup

Preparation time: 10 minutes | **Cooking time:** 25 minutes | **Serving:** 1

Ingredients

- 1 sliced garlic clove
- Grated fresh ginger: 1/6 tbsp.
- Coconut milk: 1 cup
- Vegetable broth: half cup, low-salt
- Ground turmeric: 1/3 tsp.
- Olive oil: 1/3 tsp.
- Salt & pepper, to taste
- Sliced carrots: half cup

Directions

1. In a pot, saute carrots in hot oil for 5 minutes.
2. Add turmeric, garlic and ginger and cook for 1 minute.
3. Add milk and broth, let it come to a boil.
4. Turn the heat low and simmer for 20 minutes. Stirring occasionally.
5. Turn the heat off and puree with a stick blender.
6. Adjust seasoning and serve.

Nutrition Per serving: Kcal 183 | Sodium 109 mg | Protein 3 g | Carbs 21 g | Fat 11 g | Potassium: 616 mg

17. Blueberry Lemonade Vitamin Smoothie

Preparation time: 10 minutes | **Cooking time:** 0 minute | **Serving:** 1

Ingredients

- Blueberries: 3 oz.
- ¼ lemon's juice
- Water: half cup
- Half banana, frozen
- Liquid stevia, to taste
- Lemonade vitamin powder: 1 scoop
- Spinach: 1 cup

Directions

1. In a blender, add all ingredients.
2. Pulse until smooth.
3. Serve.

Nutrition Per serving: Kcal 125 | Sodium 11.1 mg | Protein 8 g | Carbs 3.2 g | Fat 8.4 g | Potassium: 116 mg

18. Strawberry Greek Yogurt Whip

Preparation time: 10 minutes | **Cooking time:** 0 minute | **Serving:** 1

Ingredients

- No calorie sweetener, to taste
- 3 fresh strawberries
- Light whipped topping: 2 tbsp.
- Greek yogurt: half cup, no-fat

Directions

1. In a bowl, coarsely mash the strawberries and mix with yogurt and sweetener.
2. Fold the whipping topping.
3. Serve cold.

Nutrition Per serving: Kcal 24 | Sodium 13 mg | Protein 8 g | Carbs 3 g | Fat 1 g | Potassium: 47 mg

19. Light Tomato Soup

Preparation time: 10 minutes | Cooking time: 20 minutes | Serving: 1

Ingredients

- Half onion, chopped
- 4 fresh tomatoes, chopped
- 1 minced clove of garlic
- Salt & pepper, to taste
- Olive oil: ¼ tsp.
- Basil leaves: 1 tbsp., chopped
- Water, as needed

Directions

1. Sauté the onion and garlic in hot oil.
2. Add basil and tomatoes. Cook until tender.
3. Add salt and pepper, puree with a stick blender.
4. Add enough water to get the desired consistency.
5. Simmer for few minutes, serve.

Nutrition Per serving: Kcal 144 | Sodium 12.1 mg | Protein 6.7 g | Carbs 6 g | Fat 5.9 g | Potassium: 54 mg

20. Mexican Egg Puree

Preparation time: 10 minutes | Cooking time: 15 minutes | Serving: 1

Ingredients

- Greek yogurt: half tbsp., no-fat
- Canned black beans: 2 tbsp., rinsed
- Turkey sausage: 1/6 cup
- Cumin: 1/8 tsp.
- Chopped cilantro: half tbsp.
- 1 small egg
- Paprika, to taste

Directions

1. Whisk egg with spices and yogurt.
2. Cook sausage in a pan over medium flame for 5 to 6 minutes.
3. Add egg mixture and cook for 2 to 3 minutes.
4. Add cilantro and beans, cook for 1 minute.
5. Add 2 tablespoons of water and puree with a stick blender or in a food processor.
6. Serve.

Nutrition Per serving: Kcal 128 | Sodium 236 mg | Protein 12.6 g | Carbs 2.6 g | Fat 7.1 g | Potassium: 54 mg

21. Chimichurri Chicken Puree

Preparation time: 10 minutes | Cooking time: 15 minutes | Serving: 1

Ingredients

- Paprika: 1/8 tsp.
- Ground chicken: ¼ cup
- Chopped parsley: 2 tbsp.
- Apple cider vinegar: ¼ tsp.
- Cilantro: 1 tbsp.
- Dried oregano: 1/8 tsp.
- 1 clove of garlic

Directions

1. In a pan, add two tablespoons of water and heat on medium flame.
2. Add chicken, oregano and paprika; cook for 6 to 8 minutes. Add more water if necessary.
3. Add the rest of the ingredients to a food processor, pulse until smooth.
4. Add the chimichurri to the chicken. Toss well and pulse in the food processor.
5. Serve.

Nutrition Per serving: Kcal 47.6 | Sodium 81.5 mg | Protein 5.6 g | Carbs 0.5 g | Fat 2.3 g | Potassium: 54 mg

22. Turkey Tacos with Refried Beans

Preparation time: 10 minutes | Cooking time: 20 minutes | Serving: 1

Ingredients

For beans

- Pinto beans: 1/4 cup, rinsed
- Chopped cilantro: 1 tbsp.
- Chicken broth: ¼ cup, no-salt-added
- ¼ tsp., minced garlic

For turkey

- Ground turkey: ¼ cup
- Mild chili powder, cumin, garlic powder & paprika: 1/8 tsp., each

Directions

1. Sauté garlic in 2 tbsp. of hot water for 1 minute.
2. Add broth and beans. Let it come to a boil and simmer for five minutes. Mash with a masher and cook until liquid is gone.
3. Mix with cilantro.
4. In a clean pan, sauté the turkey spices for 1 minute. Add turkey with water (2 tbsp.) cook for 6 to 8 minutes. Add more water if needed.
5. Add the beans and turkey to the food processor, pulse until smooth.
6. Serve.

Nutrition Per serving: Kcal 68| Sodium 27.3 mg | Protein 10.7 g | Carbs 0.5 g | Fat 0.9 g | Potassium: 54 mg

23. Chicken & Black Bean Mole Puree

Preparation time: 10 minutes| Cooking time: 15 minutes | Serving: 1

Ingredients

- Ground chicken: ¼ cup
- Paprika, to taste
- Chicken broth: ¼ cup
- Black beans: half cup, rinsed
- Cilantro chopped: 1 tsp.
- Half garlic clove, minced
- Soaked overnight almonds: 3
- Dried oregano, cinnamon, coriander, garlic powder: 1/8 tsp., each
- Cacao powder: ¼ tsp.

Directions

1. Sauté garlic in hot water (1 tbsp.) for 1 minute.
2. Add chicken and more water if necessary; cook for 6 to 8 minutes.
3. Add the rest of the ingredients except for beans to the food processor, pulse until smooth.
4. Add sauce to the chicken with beans and stir.
5. Let it simmer for few minutes, puree with a stick blender.
6. Serve.

Nutrition Per serving: Kcal 109| Sodium 35 mg | Protein 9.5 g | Carbs 9.5 g | Fat 3.9 g | Potassium: 54 mg

24. Eggnog Protein Shake

Preparation time: 10 minutes| Cooking time: 0 minute | Serving: 1

Ingredients

- Cinnamon & nutmeg: 1/8 tsp., each
- Ice: 1 cup
- 1 protein shake vanilla
- Rum extract: half tsp.

Directions

1. In a blender, add all ingredients.
2. Pulse until smooth. Serve.

Nutrition Per serving: Kcal 162| Sodium 270 mg | Protein 30 g | Carbs 4 g | Fat 3 g | Potassium: 310 mg

25. Pumpkin Pie Protein Shake

Preparation time: 10 minutes| Cooking time: 0 minute | Serving: 1

Ingredients

- Pumpkin spice: 1/8 tsp.
- Pumpkin puree: 1/3 cup
- Vanilla protein powder: 1 scoop
- Ice: 1 cup
- Low-fat milk: 1 cup
- Granulated stevia: 1 tsp.

Directions

1. In a blender, add all ingredients.
2. Pulse until smooth. Serve.

Nutrition Per serving: Kcal 232| Sodium 214 mg | Protein 26 g | Carbs 29.7 g | Fat 1 g | Potassium: 310 mg

26. Gingerbread Cookie Protein Shake

Preparation time: 10 minutes| Cooking time: 0 minute | Serving: 1

Ingredients

- Cinnamon: 1/8 tsp.
- Ice: 1 cup
- 1 vanilla protein shake
- Maple extract: ¼ tsp.
- Ground ginger: 1/8 tsp.

Directions

1. In a blender, add all ingredients.
2. Pulse until smooth. Serve.

Nutrition Per serving: Kcal 190 | Sodium 305 mg | Protein 26 g | Carbs 9 g | Fat 3 g | Potassium: 310 mg

27. Lemon Garlic Pureed Salmon

Preparation time: 10 minutes | Cooking time: 0 minute | Serving: 1

Ingredients

- Garlic powder: ¼ tsp.
- Mayonnaise: 1/6 tbsp., low-fat
- Canned salmon: 1.67 oz.
- Lemon juice: 1/3 tsp.

Directions

1. Drain the salmon and transfer to a food processor.
2. Add the rest of the ingredients, pulse until smooth.
3. Serve.

Nutrition Per serving: Kcal 88 | Sodium 250 mg | Protein 11 g | Carbs 1 g | Fat 4 g | Potassium: 163 mg

28. Single Serve Baked Ricotta

Preparation time: 10 minutes | Cooking time: 20 minutes | Serving: 1

Ingredients

- Low-fat cheese: 1/7 cup
- Salt and pepper, to taste
- Low-fat ricotta: 3 oz.
- Fresh basil: 1 tsp., chopped
- Garlic powder: 1/8 tsp.

Directions

1. Let the oven preheat to 350 F.
2. Oil spray 1 ramekin and place on a baking tray.
3. In a bowl, mix all the ingredients. Transfer to the ramekin and bake for 15-20 minutes.

Nutrition Per serving: Kcal 144 | Sodium 213 mg | Protein 12 g | Carbs 5 g | Fat 8 g | Potassium: 106 mg

29. Creamy Shrimp Scampi

Preparation time: 10 minutes | Cooking time: 10 minutes | Serving: 1

Ingredients

- Greek yogurt: 1 tbsp., non-fat
- Half minced garlic clove
- 4 shrimps
- Parsley chopped: half tbsp.

Directions

1. In a hot pan, add shrimps and water (2 tbsp.), cook for 2 to 3 minutes.
2. Add garlic and cook for 1 minute.
3. Turn the heat off and add yogurt and parsley, puree and serve.

Nutrition Per serving: Kcal 92 | Sodium 65 mg | Protein 14 g | Carbs 0.9 g | Fat 3.7 g | Potassium: 106 mg

30. Chocolate Peanut Butter Protein Shake

Preparation time: 10 minutes | Cooking time: 0 minute | Serving: 1

Ingredients

- Chocolate protein powder: 1 scoop
- Skim milk: half cup
- Ice cubes: half cup
- Peanut butter: 1 tbsp., smooth

Directions

1. In a blender, add all ingredients.
2. Pulse until smooth. Serve.

Nutrition Per serving: Kcal 282 | Sodium 277 mg | Protein 28 g | Carbs 24.1 g | Fat 8.7 g | Potassium: 310 mg

31. Low-Fat Refried Beans

Preparation time: 10 minutes | Cooking time: 7 minutes | Serving: 1

Ingredients

- Cilantro: 1 tsp., chopped
- Pinto beans: ¼ can, rinsed
- Garlic powder, chili powder, cumin & onion powder: 1/6 tsp., each
- Vegetable broth: ¼ cup

Directions

1. In a pan, add pinto beans with a splash of water cook for 1 to 2 minutes.
2. Add the rest of the ingredients, let it come to a boil. Cook until liquid is reduced by half.
3. Mash the beans to a desired pureed consistency. Serve.

Nutrition Per serving: Kcal 85 | Sodium 211.5 mg | Protein 5.9 g | Carbs 14.3 g | Fat 0.8 g | Potassium: 209 mg

32. Pumpkin Chicken Soup

Preparation time: 15 minutes | Cooking time: 30 minutes | Serving: 1

Ingredients

- Chopped onion: 1/6 cup
- Minced garlic: half tbsp.
- Low-fat heavy cream: 1 tbsp.
- Diced celery: 1/6 cup
- Olive oil: ¼ tsp.
- Fresh cilantro: 1 tbsp., chopped
- Chicken broth: 1 cup
- Diced carrots: 1/6 cup
- Chicken breast: half cup, shredded
- Salt & pepper, to taste
- Pumpkin puree: 2.5 oz.

Directions

1. In a pot, sauté all vegetables except for garlic in hot oil for 15 minutes, till vegetables are tender.
2. Add garlic, cook for 60 seconds.
3. Add the rest of the ingredients, puree, with a stick blender.
4. Serve.

Nutrition Per serving: Kcal 275 | Sodium 189 mg | Protein 7.3 g | Carbs 3.8 g | Fat 3.9 g | Potassium: 106 mg

33. Red Pepper Enchilada Bean

Preparation time: 10 minutes | Cooking time: 10 minutes | Serving: 1

Ingredients

- Protein powder: 1 tbsp.
- Red enchilada sauce: 1 ½ tbsp.
- Canned black beans: half cup, rinsed
- Roasted red pepper (jarred): 2 tbsp., chopped & optional
- Chicken broth: 2 tbsp.

Directions

1. In a pan, add red pepper, enchilada sauce (2 tbsp.) and bean on medium flame.
2. Cook for few minutes, add broth cook for few minutes.
3. Puree with a stick blender.
4. Take it out on a serving plate, let it cool slightly.
5. Add the rest of the ingredients, mix and serve.

Nutrition Per serving: Kcal 187 | Sodium 729 mg | Protein 19 g | Carbs 25 g | Fat 1 g | Potassium: 414 mg

34. Green Protein Smoothie

Preparation time: 10 minutes | Cooking time: 0 minute | Serving: 1

Ingredients

- Half frozen banana
- Coconut water: half cup
- Lemonade vitamin powder: 1 scoop
- Fresh spinach: half cup
- 1/4 avocado
- Pineapple chunks: 1/4 cup, frozen

Directions

1. In a blender, add all ingredients.
2. Pulse until smooth. Serve.

Nutrition Per serving: Kcal 193| Sodium 109 mg | Protein 16 g | Carbs 8 g | Fat 4.1 g | Potassium: 110 mg

35. White Bean Soup

Preparation time: 10 minutes | Cooking time: 30 minutes | Serving: 1

Ingredients

- Half carrots, chopped
- Oregano: ¼ tsp.
- 1/4 onion, chopped
- Half minced garlic cloves, minced
- Paprika: 1/8 tsp.
- Chicken broth: 1 cup, no-salt-added
- Green beans: half cup
- Half celery sticks, chopped
- Tomato paste: ¼ tsp.
- White beans: ¼ can
- Salt & pepper, to taste
- Canned tomatoes: ¼ can
- Half bay leave

Directions

1. Saute celery, onion and carrots in a splash of water for ten minutes.
2. Add paprika, garlic and oregano, cook for 45 to 60 seconds.
3. Add the rest of the ingredients, stir well and let it come to a boil.
4. Turn the heat low and simmer for 20 minutes, covered.
5. Adjust seasoning and puree with a stick blender.
6. Serve.

Nutrition Per serving: Kcal 191| Sodium 238 mg | Protein 9 g | Carbs 33 g | Fat 4 g | Potassium: 402 mg

36. Carrot Lemonade Smoothie

Preparation time: 10 minutes | Cooking time: 30 minutes | Serving: 1

Ingredients

- 1/4 frozen banana
- Parsley: 1 tbsp., chopped
- Peeled ginger: ¼" piece
- 1 lemon's juice
- Half carrot
- Water: ¼ cup
- Lemonade Vitamin Powder: 1 scoop

Directions

1. In a blender, add all ingredients.
2. Pulse until smooth. Serve.

Nutrition Per serving: Kcal 160| Sodium 78.9 mg | Protein 13.9 g | Carbs 6 g | Fat 3.8 g | Potassium: 111 mg

37. Sweet Potato Puree

Preparation time: 10 minutes | Cooking time: 10 minutes | Serving: 1

Ingredients

- Butter: 1 tbsp.
- Cinnamon: ¼ tsp.
- Salt: half tsp.
- 1 sweet potato
- Orange juice: 2 tbsp.
- Nutmeg: ¼ tsp.
- Stevia: half-packet
- Black pepper, to taste
- 0% milk: 1 tbsp.

Directions

1. Trim the potato and wrap it in parchment paper.
2. Microwave for 5 to 6 minutes. Cut the potato and transfer the soft flesh to a food processor.
3. Add the rest of the ingredients, pulse until smooth.
4. Serve.

Nutrition Per serving: Kcal 224| Sodium 92.1 mg | Protein 7.3 g | Carbs 17.3 g | Fat 6 g | Potassium: 265 mg

38. Buffalo Ranch Chicken

Preparation time: 10 minutes | Cooking time: 0 minute | Serving: 1

Ingredients

- Sour cream: ¼ cup, low-fat
- Canned chicken: 1 can
- Cream cheese: 4 oz., low-fat
- Hot sauce, to taste
- Mexican shredded cheese: ¼ packet
- Ranch seasoning: half-packet

Directions
1. In a food processor, add all ingredients.
2. Pulse until smooth, serve.

Nutrition Per serving: Kcal 209 | Sodium 111 mg | Protein 21 g | Carbs 4.9 g | Fat 8.1 g | Potassium: 287 mg

39. Chili Puree

Preparation time: 10 minutes | Cooking time: 40 minutes | Serving: 1

Ingredients
- Chili beans: ¼ can
- Chili seasoning, to taste
- 1/4 green pepper
- Turkey meat: half cup
- Diced tomatoes: ¼ can
- Ketchup: ¼ tsp.
- Pinto beans: ¼ can
- Tomato paste: 2 tbsp.

Directions
1. In a pan, add turkey and green pepper. Cook until done.
2. Add the rest of the ingredients, cook for 30-40 minutes.
3. Puree with a stick blender, serve.

Nutrition Per serving: Kcal 267 | Sodium 320 mg | Protein 19.9 g | Carbs 12 g | Fat 12.9 g | Potassium: 276 mg

40. No Chew Cheeseburgers

Preparation time: 10 minutes | Cooking time: 20 minutes | Serving: 1

Ingredients
- 1 minced garlic clove
- Olive oil: ¼ tsp.
- Worchestershire, to taste
- Ground meat of your choice: half cup
- Onion chopped: 1 tbsp.
- Salt & pepper, to taste

Directions
1. In a pan, saute garlic and onion in hot oil.
2. Add meat and cook until done; drain any oil.
3. Add the rest of the ingredients. Cook for a few minutes more.
4. Puree with a stick blender, serve.

Nutrition Per serving: Kcal 218 | Sodium 210 mg | Protein 20 g | Carbs 8 g | Fat 7 g | Potassium: 298 mg

41. Italian Chicken Puree

Preparation time: 10 minutes | Cooking time: 5 minutes | Serving: 1

Ingredients
- Italian seasoning: 1 tsp.
- Tomato sauce: 1 ½ tbsp.
- Canned chicken: ¼ cup
- Salt & pepper, to taste

Directions
1. In a bowl, add the ingredients.
2. Puree with a stick blender.
3. Microwave for 30 seconds. Serve.

Nutrition Per serving: Kcal 106 | Sodium 656 mg | Protein 13 g | Carbs 3 g | Fat 4 g | Potassium: 181 mg

42. Ricotta & White Bean Puree

Preparation time: 10 minutes | Cooking time: 5 minutes | Serving: 1

Ingredients
- Chopped fresh parsley: 2 tbsp.
- Fat-free ricotta: ¾ cup
- Cannellini beans: ¼ can, with liquid
- Half minced garlic clove

Directions
1. In a pot, add beans with liquid and garlic.
2. Let it come to a boil, turn the heat low and simmer for 3 to 4 minutes.
3. Take it out in a bowl, mix with the rest of the ingredients.
4. Puree with a stick blender. Serve.

Nutrition Per serving: Kcal 60 | Sodium 45 mg | Protein 4.7 g | Carbs 9.5 g | Fat 0.4 g | Potassium: 102 mg

43. Ginger Garlic Tofu Puree

Preparation time: 10 minutes | Cooking time: 10 minutes | Serving: 1

Ingredients

- Firm tofu: 4 oz., cubed
- Minced ginger: ¼ tsp.
- Coconut aminos: ¼ tsp.
- Half minced garlic clove

Directions

1. In a pan, add all ingredients (except for tofu) with water (1/4 cup).
2. Let it come to a boil; add tofu. Cook for 3 to 4 minutes.
3. Add more water if needed. Puree with a stick blender.
4. Serve.

Nutrition Per serving: Kcal 61 | Sodium 43 mg | Protein 6.9 g | Carbs 2.8 g | Fat 3.4 g | Potassium: 102 mg

44. Moroccan Fish Puree

Preparation time: 10 minutes | Cooking time: 10 minutes | Serving: 1

Ingredients

- Half clove of minced garlic
- Paprika, cinnamon, turmeric & cumin: 1/8 tsp., each
- Coconut lite milk: ¼ cup
- Apple cider vinegar: ¼ tsp.
- Chopped fresh cilantro: 1 tbsp.
- Whitefish fillets: 4 oz.
- Canned chickpeas: ¼ cup, rinsed

Directions

1. In a pan, add dry spices and cook for 1 minute.
2. Add garlic, vinegar and water (2 tbsp.), cook for 1 to 2 minutes.
3. Add the rest of the ingredients, cook on high.
4. Let it come to a boil, turn the heat low and simmer for 4 to 6 minutes.
5. Turn the heat off, add cilantro. Puree with a stick blender.

Nutrition Per serving: Kcal 67 | Sodium 33 mg | Protein 7 g | Carbs 6.8 g | Fat 1.2 g | Potassium: 113 mg

45. Sesame Tuna Salad Puree

Preparation time: 10 minutes | Cooking time: 0 minute | Serving: 1

Ingredients

- Tahini: ¼ tsp.
- Chopped parsley: 1 tsp.
- Apple cider vinegar: ¼ tsp.
- Coconut aminos: 1/8 tsp.
- Greek yogurt: 2 tbsp., low-fat
- Sesame seeds: ¼ tsp.
- Canned light tuna: 4 oz., in water

Directions

1. Whisk all ingredients except for fish.
2. Break the tuna and add to the mixture.
3. Puree and serve.

Nutrition Per serving: Kcal 78 | Sodium 209 mg | Protein 11.7 g | Carbs 1.3 g | Fat 3.4 g | Potassium: 132 mg

46. Caribbean Pork Puree

Preparation time: 10 minutes | Cooking time: 5 minutes | Serving: 1

Ingredients

- Dried thyme: 1/8 tsp.
- Dried parsley: 1/8 tsp.
- Chopped fresh cilantro: 1 tsp.
- Allspice: 1/8 tsp.
- Paprika: 1/8 tsp.
- Garlic powder: 1/8 tsp.
- Apple cider vinegar: ¼ tsp.
- Ground pork: half cup
- Canned black beans: ¼ cup

Directions

1. In a pan, add all dry spices and herbs cook for 1 minute.
2. Add pork with water (2 tbsp.) on high heat. Cook for 4 to 5 minutes, until done.
3. Add more water if needed.
4. Add beans and vinegar, cook for 1 to 2 minutes.
5. Turn the heat off, add cilantro.
6. Pulse until smooth. Serve.

Nutrition Per serving: Kcal 65 | Sodium 29 mg | Protein 9.8 g | Carbs 2.6 g | Fat 1.8 g | Potassium: 121 mg

47. Rosemary Chicken with Blue Cheese

Preparation time: 10 minutes | Cooking time: 10 minutes | Serving: 1

Ingredients

- Ground chicken: 4 oz.
- Canned chickpeas: ¼ cup, rinsed
- Half minced garlic clove
- Toasted sunflower seeds: 1/8 tsp., unsalted
- Blue cheese, crumbled: 1/4 tsp., low-fat
- Apple cider vinegar: 1/8 tsp.
- Greek yogurt: 2 tbsp., low-fat
- Fresh rosemary: 1 tsp., chopped

Directions

1. In a pan, add garlic with water (2 tbsp.) cook for 1 minute.
2. Add chicken and cook for 6 to 8 minutes. Add more water if the pan is dry.
3. Add chickpeas and rosemary, cook for 2 to 3 minutes. Turn the heat off
4. Add the rest of the ingredients to a bowl and mix. Transfer to the chicken mixture.
5. Puree and serve.

Nutrition Per serving: Kcal 135 | Sodium 67 mg | Protein 10.3 g | Carbs 3 g | Fat 2 g | Potassium: 183 mg

48. Mediterranean Chicken Puree

Preparation time: 10 minutes | Cooking time: 10 minutes | Serving: 1

Ingredients

- Tahini: ¼ tsp.
- Parsley: 1 tsp., chopped
- Za'atar spice: ¼ tsp.
- Ground chicken: 3 oz.
- Canned chickpeas: ¼ cup, rinsed

Directions

1. In a pan, add chicken and water (2 tbsp.), cook for 5 to 7 minutes on medium flame.
2. Add the rest of the ingredients to a bowl, mix and add to the chicken.
3. Cook until heated through.
4. Puree until smooth, serve.

Nutrition Per serving: Kcal 89 | Sodium 127 mg | Protein 9 g | Carbs 2 g | Fat 4 g | Potassium: 103 mg

49. Pureed Chicken Breast Salad

Preparation time: 10 minutes | Cooking time: 0 minute | Serving: 1

Ingredients

- Greek yogurt: 1 tbsp., low-fat
- Salt & black pepper
- Half chicken breast, cooked
- Mayonnaise: 1 tbsp., low-fat
- Onion powder: 1/8 tsp.

Directions

1. In a food processor, pulse the chicken until smooth.
2. Mix with the rest of the ingredients.
3. Serve.

Nutrition Per serving: Kcal 97 | Sodium 67 mg | Protein 14 g | Carbs 2.9 g | Fat 1.2 g | Potassium: 134 mg

50. Chicken & Sweet Potato Puree

Preparation time: 10 minutes | Cooking time: 20 minutes | Serving: 1

Ingredients

- Half peeled sweet potato, cubed
- Chicken breast half, cooked

Directions

1. In a pan, add sweet potato with water.
2. Cook for 10-15 minutes, until tender. Drain all but some liquid.
3. Mash with a masher.
4. In a food processor, pulse the chicken until smooth. Add mashed sweet potato with the liquid.
5. Pulse until smooth.
6. Adjust seasoning with salt and pepper. Serve.

Nutrition Per serving: Kcal 45 | Sodium 10 mg | Protein 4 g | Carbs 3 g | Fat 1.9 g | Potassium: 35 mg

51. Banana, Tofu & Pear Puree

Preparation time: 10 minutes | Cooking time: 0 minute | Serving: 1

Ingredients

- 1/4 pear, peeled & chopped
- Tofu: 2 oz.
- Half banana

Directions

1. In a food processor, add all ingredients, pulse until smooth.

2. Serve.

Nutrition Per serving: Kcal 56| Sodium 3 mg | Protein 4.9 g | Carbs 3.1 g | Fat 1 g | Potassium: 31 mg

52. Cheesy Cauliflower Puree

Preparation time: 10 minutes| Cooking time: 15 minutes | Serving: 1

Ingredients

- Cream: 2 tbsp., low-fat
- Salt & pepper, to taste
- Butter: half tsp.
- Cauliflower florets: half cup
- Low-fat cheese: 1 oz.

Directions

1. In a bowl, add florets with butter and cream. Microwave for 4-6 minutes.
2. Mix and microwave for 4-6 minutes more.
3. Pulse in a food processor with cheese. Adjust seasoning and serve.

Nutrition Per serving: Kcal 146| Sodium 109 mg | Protein 6 g | Carbs 4 g | Fat 11 g | Potassium: 209 mg

53. Basic Oatmeal

Preparation time: 10 minutes| Cooking time: 10 minutes | Serving: 1

Ingredients

- Skim milk: half cup
- Cinnamon: ¼ tsp.
- Water: half cup
- Low-fat sweetener, to taste
- Rolled oats: half cup, old-fashioned
- Kosher salt, a pinch

Directions

1. In a pan, add all ingredients, cook until done.
2. Pulse until smooth.
3. Serve.

Nutrition Per serving: Kcal 220| Sodium 180 mg | Protein 12 g | Carbs 14 g | Fat 5 g | Potassium: 130 mg

54. Peppermint Shake

Preparation time: 10 minutes| Cooking time: 0 minute | Serving: 1

Ingredients

- Ice cubes, as needed
- Vanilla pudding: half pack
- Peppermint extract: ¼ tsp.
- Coldwater: 1 cup
- Vanilla extract: 1/8 tsp.

Directions

1. In a blender, add all ingredients.
2. Pulse until smooth. Serve.

Nutrition Per serving: Kcal 93| Sodium 78 mg | Protein 15 g | Carbs 6 g | Fat 0.1 g | Potassium: 91 mg

55. Lemon Crystal Shake

Preparation time: 10 minutes| Cooking time: 0 minute | Serving: 1

Ingredients

- 4 ice cubes
- Vanilla Shake: half pack
- 1 Crystal Light drink, lemon-flavored

Directions

1. As per the pack's instructions, prepare the light drink.
2. In the vanilla shake, add the lemon drink instead of water. Transfer to a blender, pulse until combined.
3. Serve.

Nutrition Per serving: Kcal 95| Sodium 56 mg | Protein 15 g | Carbs 6 g | Fat 0 g | Potassium: 87 mg

56. Orange Tea

Preparation time: 10 minutes| Cooking time: 0 minute | Serving: 1

Ingredients

- Nutmeg, a pinch
- Water: 1 cup
- Instant tea: 1 tsp.
- Orangeade fruit drink: 1 pack
- Cinnamon, a pinch

Directions

1. In a blender, add all ingredients.

2. Pulse until smooth and combined.
3. Serve.

Nutrition Per serving: Kcal 70 | Sodium 56 mg | Protein 15 g | Carbs 1 g | Fat 0 g | Potassium: 15 mg

57. Pureed Vegetable

Preparation time: 10 minutes | Cooking time: 0 minute | Serving: 1

Ingredients

- Low-fat milk, as needed
- Cauliflower florets, half cup
- 1 small carrot, chopped
- Butter: 1 tsp

Directions

1. Steam the vegetables.
2. Transfer to a food processor, add the rest of the ingredients.
3. Add water as required, pulse until smooth.
4. Adjust seasoning, serve.

Nutrition Per serving: Kcal 77 | Sodium 35 mg |

Protein 6 g | Carbs 3.2 g | Fat 2 g | Potassium: 76 mg

Chapter 6: Stage 3: Semi-Solid/Soft foods

What you CAN eat	What NOT to eat
• Any lean meats, including ground beef • Any seafood & fish • Eggs • Cottage cheese • Greek yogurt • Beans • Protein bars • Non-starchy vegetables • Any fruits	• Steak • Peas • Potatoes • Corn • Starches: bread, pasta, rice, oatmeal, cerealFried foods • Refinedsugar/desserts • <u>LIMIT</u>: nuts & nut butters

This phase of your diet will begin in 7-8 weeks after the surgery. During this period, soft things to consume include:

Canned tuna, or crab or chicken

- Lean meats such as slow-cooked pork or chicken
- Refried beans, mashed chickpeas, tofu, or mashed lentils
- Smooth, low-fat cheeses
- Chili or stew, trout, salmon or flaky fish
- Soft fruits like peaches, avocados melons
- Overcooked veggies like squash, cauliflower, mushrooms or zucchini,

Keep drinking fluids in between meals, but follow the 30/30 rule: don't drink for 30 minutes before or after the meal. Maintain the daily protein and mineral intake.

- Meals should include 75% protein and just a little quantity of carbs and lipids.
- Check food labels to see how many calories, proteins, fats are in each item.
- Eggs (scrambled or soft boiled), tofu, stewed chicken, well-cooked vegetables, baked fish, sugar-free low-fat yogurt, and soft fruits are examples of soft meals. Take tiny pieces and chew them gently. Food should be chewed until a liquid, or blended consistency is achieved. You're using the tongue to replace the blender.

Drinking drinks with your meals is never a good idea.

1. High Protein Deviled Egg & Bacon

Preparation time: 10 minutes | Cooking time: 0 minute | Serving: 8

Ingredients

- Canned chickpeas: 3 tbsp., rinsed
- 8 hard-boiled Eggs
- Dill: 2 tbsp., chopped
- 2 slices of cooked bacon, crumbled
- Greek yogurt: half cup
- Dijon mustard: 1 tbsp.
- Paprika: ¼ tsp.

Directions

1. Slice the egg in half lengthwise.
2. Take the yolk out in a food processor, add the rest of the ingredients except for egg white, bacon and paprika. Pulse until combined & smooth.
3. Spoon the mixture into the egg white.
4. Serve with bacon on top.

Nutrition Per serving (2 halves): Kcal 77 | Sodium 182 mg | Protein 8 g | Carbs 2.5 g | Fat 2 g | Potassium: 76 mg

2. Baked Ricotta Florentine

Preparation time: 10 minutes | Cooking time: 20 minutes | Serving: 4

Ingredients

- Sun-dried tomatoes: 2 tbsp., chopped
- Parmesan cheese: 2 tbsp., grated
- Fresh spinach: ¼ cup, chopped
- Part-skim ricotta cheese: 8 oz.
- Mozzarella cheese: half cup, low-fat & shredded

Directions

1. Let the oven preheat to 350 F. Oil spray 4 ramekins.
2. Oil spray a pan and place on medium flame.
3. Cook spinach until it wilts.
4. In a bowl, mix cheeses with tomatoes and spinach. Spoon into prepared ramekins.
5. Bake for 15 to 20 minutes.

Nutrition Per serving: Kcal 178 | Sodium 208 mg | Protein 6.9 g | Carbs 4 g | Fat 8.3 g | Potassium: 145 mg

3. Spinach Soup With Lemon

Preparation time: 10 minutes | Cooking time: 20 minutes | Serving: 4

Ingredients

- Olive oil: ¾ tbsp.
- Vegetable broth: 3 cups, low-sodium
- 1 lemon's juice
- 1 sliced white onion
- Peeled potatoes: half lb., chunks
- Frozen spinach: 1 lb., thawed & drained
- 1 sliced garlic clove
- Salt & pepper, to taste

Directions

1. Saute garlic and onion in hot oil for 3 minutes.
2. Add broth, potatoes and let it come to a boil. Turn the heat low and simmer for ten minutes, till potatoes are tender.
3. Add spinach, cook, until it softens.
4. Turn the heat off and puree with a stick blender. Adjust seasoning.
5. Add lemon juice and Serve.

Nutrition Per serving: Kcal 103 | Sodium 378 mg | Protein 5 g | Carbs 16 g | Fat 3 g | Potassium: 639 mg

4. Scrambled Eggs With Black Bean

Preparation time: 10 minutes | Cooking time: 20 minutes | Serving: 4

Ingredients

For Eggs

- Salt & pepper: half tsp., each
- 4 egg

Black Bean Puree

- Whey protein powder: 4 tbsp., unflavored
- Green enchilada sauce: 12 tbsp.
- Canned black beans: 2 cup, rinsed
- Chicken broth: 8 tbsp.

Directions

1. In a pan, add beans on medium flame.
2. Add enchilada sauce, cook for 2 minutes. Add broth puree with a stick blender.
3. Take it out in a bowl. Cool slightly.
4. Add protein powder and mix.
5. Oil spray a pan and add whisked eggs on medium flame.
6. Add salt and pepper, cook to scramble. Serve with black bean puree.

Nutrition Per serving: Kcal 118 | Sodium 356 mg | Protein 11 g | Carbs 6 g | Fat 5 g | Potassium: 467 mg

5. Pork Taco Soup

Preparation time: 10 minutes | Cooking time: 20 minutes | Serving: 8

Ingredients

- Paprika, onion powder & garlic powder: half tsp., each
- Pinto beans & black beans: half cup each
- Dried oregano: ¼ tsp.
- Cumin: 1 tsp.
- Ground lean pork: half lb.
- Chopped cilantro: ¼ cup
- Chicken broth: 1 cup, low-sodium
- Chopped zucchini: 1 cup
- Olive oil: 1 tsp.
- Greek yogurt: ¼ cup, low-fat

Directions

1. In a pan, add dry spices. Cook for 2 to 3 minutes.
2. Add oil and cook for 30 seconds.
3. Add pork, cook for 5 to 7 minutes.
4. Add broth, beans and zucchini. Let it come to a boil, turn the heat low and simmer until zucchini is tender, for 4 to 5 minutes.
5. Pulse with a stick blender until smooth. Serve with yogurt and cilantro on top.

Nutrition Per serving: Kcal 99.4 | Sodium 35.7 mg | Protein 10 g | Carbs 8.6 g | Fat 3.3 g | Potassium: 467 mg

6. Greek Yogurt Parfait

Preparation time: 10 minutes | Cooking time: 0 minute | Serving: 2

Ingredients

- 4 packets of Truvia
- Greek yogurt: 20 oz., low-fat
- Frozen blueberries: 4 tbsp.

Directions

1. Microwave the blueberries for 30 seconds.
2. Mix the yogurt with sweetener. Mix with blueberries. Serve.

Nutrition Per serving: Kcal 80 | Sodium 51 mg | Protein 14 g | Carbs 7 g | Fat 1 g | Potassium: 200 mg

7. Banana Spinach Protein Smoothie

Preparation time: 10 minutes | Cooking time: 0 minute | Serving: 1

Ingredients

- Low-fat Greek yogurt: 2/3 cup
- Vanilla protein powder: 1 scoop
- Half banana
- Fresh spinach: ¾ cup
- Almond butter: 1 tbsp.
- Water: ¾ cup

Directions

1. In a blender, add all ingredients.
2. Pulse until smooth, serve.

Nutrition Per serving: Kcal 109 | Sodium 76 mg | Protein 8.9 g | Carbs 3 g | Fat 2.9 g | Potassium: 108 mg

8. Creamsicle

Preparation time: 10 minutes | Cooking time: 0 minute | Serving: 2

Ingredients

- Nonfat yogurt: 4 oz.
- Vanilla protein powder: 1 scoop
- Splenda: 1 packet
- Water: 4 oz.
- Mandarin oranges: half cup
- Skim milk: 2 ice cubes

Directions

1. In a blender, add all ingredients.
2. Pulse until smooth, serve.

Nutrition Per serving: Kcal 112 | Sodium 87 mg | Protein 9 g | Carbs 2.8 g | Fat 1.9 g | Potassium: 104 mg

9. Mocha Java

Preparation time: 10 minutes | Cooking time: 0 minute | Serving: 2

Ingredients

- 1 packet of Splenda
- Chocolate protein powder: 1 scoop
- Skim milk: 10 oz.
- Skim milk: 2 ice cubes
- Instant decaf coffee: 1 tbsp.

Directions

1. In a blender, add all ingredients.
2. Pulse until smooth, serve.

Nutrition Per serving: Kcal 112 | Sodium 87 mg | Protein 9 g | Carbs 2.8 g | Fat 1.9 g | Potassium: 104 mg

10. Berry Bomb

Preparation time: 10 minutes | Cooking time: 0 minute | Serving: 2

Ingredients

- Whey protein powder: 1 scoop
- Cran-grape juice: half cup, diet
- Skim milk: half cup
- Frozen blueberries: half cup

Directions

1. In a blender, add all ingredients.
2. Pulse until smooth, serve.

Nutrition Per serving: Kcal 121 | Sodium 89 mg | Protein 5.9 g | Carbs 2.1 g | Fat 2 g | Potassium: 103.2 mg

11. Berry Avocado Smoothie

Preparation time: 10 minutes | Cooking time: 0 minute | Serving: 2

Ingredients

- Blueberries: ¼ cup
- Sweetener: 1 tsp.
- Half avocado
- Strawberries: 1 cup
- Greek yogurt: half cup, low-fat
- Lowfat milk: half cup

Directions

1. In a blender add all ingredients.
2. Pulse until smooth, serve.

Nutrition Per serving: Kcal 352 | Sodium 154 mg | Protein 22 g | Carbs 39 g | Fat 16 g | Potassium: 109 mg

12. Tuscan White Bean Soup

Preparation time: 15 minutes | Cooking time: 45 minute | Serving: 3-4

Ingredients

- 1 large zucchini, diced
- 1 celery stalk, diced
- Olive oil: 1 tbsp.
- 2 small carrots, diced
- Chicken broth: 2 ½ cups
- Kale: 1 ½ cups, chopped
- 1 can of (15 oz.) Fire-roasted tomatoes: ¾ can, diced
- Half yellow onion, diced
- 1 can of (15 oz.) Cannellini beans: ¾ can
- 2 small cloves of garlic, minced
- Tomato paste: 1 ½ tbsp.

Seasonings

- Salt, pepper & red pepper flakes: to taste
- Dried thyme, basil & oregano: ¾ tbsp., each

Directions

1. In a Dutch oven, sauté vegetables except for zucchini and garlic for 4 to 5 minutes in hot oil.
2. Add zucchini and garlic, cook for 3 minutes.
3. Add the rest of the ingredients (do not add kale yet). Stir well. Cook on low for half an hour, covered.
4. Turn the heat off and add kale; stir.
5. Make it into chunky soup with a stick blender, serve.

Nutrition Per serving: Kcal 121 | Sodium 923 mg | Protein 4.7 g | Carbs 18 g | Fat 4 g | Potassium: 187 mg

13. Chocolate Cherry Shake

Preparation time: 10 minutes | Cooking time: 0 minute | Serving: 2

Ingredients

- Coldwater: 2 cup
- Sugar-free chocolate shake: 2 packets
- Cherry juice: 4 tbsp., unsweetened

Directions

1. In a jug, add all ingredients, stir well
2. Serve.

Nutrition Per serving: Kcal 108 | Sodium 281 mg | Protein 15.1 g | Carbs 10.2 g | Fat 1.2 g | Potassium: 187 mg

14. Turkey Kale Meatballs

Preparation time: 15 minutes | Cooking time: 35 minutes | Serving: 4

Ingredients

- Baby kale: 1 ½ cups, chopped
- Apple cider vinegar: 1 tsp.
- Garlic powder: 1 tsp.
- Parmesan cheese: 1 tbsp., low-fat
- Ground lean turkey: 1 lb.
- 1 egg
- Parsley & dill chopped: 2 tbsp., each
- Greek yogurt: ¼ cup, low-fat

Directions

1. Let the oven preheat to 350 F and oil spray a baking sheet.
2. In a bowl, mix egg, turkey, kale and parmesan. Make it into 16 balls.
3. Bake for 25 to 30 minutes on the baking sheet, flipping halfway through.
4. Add the rest of the ingredients to a bowl with hot water (1 tbsp.).
5. Drizzle over meatballs and serve.

Nutrition Per serving: Kcal 172 | Sodium 77 mg | Protein 32 g | Carbs 1.6 g | Fat 4.2 g | Potassium: 187 mg

15. Buffalo Chicken Meatballs

Preparation time: 15 minutes | Cooking time: 20 minutes | Serving: 4

Ingredients

- Ground Chicken: half pound
- Cream Cheese: 2 tbsp., low-fat softened
- Pepper Jack Cheese: ¼ cup, low-fat, Shredded
- Buffalo Sauce: ¼ cup
- Cheddar Cheese: ¼ cup, low-fat, Shredded

Directions

1. Let the oven preheat to 350 F.
2. Add all ingredients to a bowl and mix, make into mini meatballs.
3. Place in a baking dish, cover with foil.
4. Bake for 15 to 20 minutes.
5. Serve.

Nutrition Per 2 balls: Kcal 161 | Sodium 599 mg | Protein 14 g | Carbs 1 g | Fat 12 g | Potassium: 306 mg

16. Ricotta Scrambled Eggs

Preparation time: 10 minutes | Cooking time: 7 minutes | Serving: 2

Ingredients

- Ricotta: half cup, softened
- 2 eggs
- Fresh chives: 1 tbsp., chopped
- Salt & pepper, to taste
- Milk: half cup

Directions

1. In a bowl, whisk eggs with milk, salt and pepper.
2. Cook eggs to scramble in the halftime mix in ricotta. Cook for 1 minute.
3. Serve with fresh chives on top.

Nutrition Per 2 balls: Kcal 201 | Sodium 150 mg | Protein 14 g | Carbs 5 g | Fat 12 g | Potassium: 109 mg

17. Zucchini Soup

Preparation time: 15 minutes | Cooking time: 35 minute | Serving: 6

Ingredients

- Chicken broth: 3 cups
- 1 yellow onion, chopped
- Celery salt: ¼ tsp.
- Low-fat cream: half cup
- 2 minced cloves of garlic
- Butter: 1 tbsp.
- Dried thyme: ¼ tsp.
- Cayenne, a pinch
- Black pepper: ¼ tsp.
- Dried rosemary: ¼ tsp.
- Shredded cheddar cheese: 1 cup, low-fat
- 2 russet potatoes, peeled & diced
- Kosher salt: ¼ tsp.
- Peeled zucchini chunks: 5 cups
- Soy sauce: 1 tbsp.

Directions

1. In a pot, saute onion in butter for 5 minutes. Add garlic and cook for 60 seconds.
2. Add seasoning and zucchini, cook for 5 minutes.
3. Add soy sauce, broth and potatoes.
4. Let it come to a boil, turn the heat low and simmer for 20-25 minutes, partially covered.
5. Turn the heat off, purree with a stick blender. Serve with cheese on top.

Nutrition Per Serving: Kcal 226 | Sodium 963 mg | Protein 14 g | Carbs 20 g | Fat 13 g | Potassium: 738 mg

18. Crockpot Curry Chicken

Preparation time: 10 minutes | Cooking time: 4 hours | Serving: 6

Ingredients

- Salt & pepper: ¼ tsp., each
- Curry powder: 3 tbsp.
- 1 sliced yellow onion
- 1 lb. Chicken thighs: boneless, skinless
- 1 red bell pepper, sliced thinly
- Frozen peas: 1 cup
- 1 carrot, diced
- Chicken broth: 1 cup, low-sodium
- Garlic minced: 1 tsp.
- Light coconut milk: 2 cups
- Cauliflower Rice: 3 cups
- Corn starch: 1 tbsp.
- Water: 1 tbsp.

Directions

1. Season the chicken with salt and pepper.
2. In a crockpot, add chicken, milk, broth and vegetables. Stir and cook for 4 hours on low.
3. Take the chicken out and shred finely.
4. In a bowl, add cornstarch and water in equal parts. Add to the crockpot and stir; cook for ten minutes.
5. Add the shredded chicken back in the pot.
6. Serve with cauliflower rice.

Nutrition Per Serving: Kcal 287 | Sodium 666 mg | Protein 21 g | Carbs 16 g | Fat 11.9 g | Potassium: 323 mg

19. Baked Fish with Almond Chutney

Preparation time: 10 minutes | Cooking time: 30 minutes | Serving: 8

Ingredients

- Sliced almonds: half cup
- Olive oil: 1 tbsp.
- Coriander: 1 tsp.
- Flaky white fish: 1 lb.
- Lemon juice: 2 tsp.
- diced tomatoes: half cup

Directions

1. Let the oven preheat to 375 F.
2. Mix lemon juice and olive oil in a baking dish.
3. Add fish and coat well, bake for 15 to 20 minutes.
4. Add the rest of the ingredients to a food processor, pulse until chunky. Pour over fish and bake for 2 to 3 minutes more.

Nutrition Per Serving: Kcal 136 | Sodium 67 mg | Protein 17 g | Carbs 2.1 g | Fat 6.9 g | Potassium: 123 mg

20. Cranberry, Sage & Gruyere Turkey Meatballs

Preparation time: 10 minutes | Cooking time: 20 minutes | Serving: 16

Ingredients

- Breadcrumbs plain: 1/3 cup
- Sugar-free dried cranberries: 1/3 cup
- 1 egg
- Lean ground turkey: 1 pound
- Black pepper: 1/8 tsp.
- Shredded gruyere: 1/3 cup
- Salt, a pinch
- Dried sage: ¼ tsp.

Directions

1. Let the oven preheat to 350 F. Oil spray a baking pan.
2. In a bowl, mix all the ingredients. Make into 1 ½ oz. balls.
3. Bake for 15 to 20 minutes. Serve.

Nutrition for 3 meatballs: Kcal 172 | Sodium 185.1 mg | Protein 21.5 g | Carbs 11.7 g | Fat 6.9 g | Potassium: 301 mg

21. Juicy Jelly/Jello Pots

Preparation time: 20 minutes | Cooking time: 0 minutes | Serving: 4

Ingredients

- Fresh berries: 1 ½ cups
- Sugar-free raspberry jello crystals: 2 ½ cups
- Prepared custard: 4 oz., low-sugar & low-fat
- Protein powder: 1 scoop

Directions

1. Dissolve the jelly in one cup of boiling water, cool slightly and add protein powder.
2. Mix well and divide into 4 serving glasses. Let it chill.
3. Serve each serving glass with custard and fruits on top.

Nutrition Per Serving: Kcal 69 | Sodium 67 mg | Protein 6.9 g | Carbs 8.4 g | Fat 0.9 g | Potassium: 89 mg

22. Spinach & Feta Bake

Preparation time: 10 minutes | Cooking time: 35 minutes | Serving: 3

Ingredients

- 1 yellow onion, diced
- Crumbled feta cheese: 4 oz., low-fat
- Skim Milk: 1/3 cup
- Frozen chopped spinach: 24 oz., (thawed & squeezed)
- Soybean oil: 3 tbsp.
- Cayenne, a pinch
- Salt & pepper, to taste
- Fresh dill: ¼ cup, chopped
- 4 eggs, whisked
- All-purpose flour: 1 cup

Directions

1. Let the oven preheat to 350 F., oil spray a 9" pie dish.
2. Sauté the onion in hot oil for 8 minutes.
3. Add feta, spinach, dill, salt, cayenne and pepper. Cook for 1 to 2 minutes pour in the pie dish.
4. Add the rest of the ingredients to a bowl, pour over the spinach mixture.
5. Bake for 25 to 30 minutes. Slice and serve.

Nutrition Per Serving: Kcal 200 | Sodium 450 mg | Protein 9 g | Carbs 18 g | Fat 11 g | Potassium: 179 mg

23. Soft Crab Salad

Preparation time: 10 minutes | Cooking time: 0 minutes | Serving: 2

Ingredients

- Dried dill: 1/4 tsp.
- Imitation crab: 8 oz.
- Protein powder: 2 scoop
- Light mayonnaise: 4 tbsp.
- Seafood seasoning: ¼ tsp.

Directions

1. Shred the crab meat. Mix with the rest of the ingredients.
2. Serve.

Nutrition Per Serving: Kcal 118 | Sodium 448 mg | Protein 13 g | Carbs 8 g | Fat 5 g | Potassium: 89 mg

24. Spicy Vegetarian Chili

Preparation time: 20 minutes | Cooking time: 30 minutes | Serving: 10

Ingredients

- 1 sweet onion, large & diced
- 1 green & 1 red bell pepper, diced
- Water: 3 cups
- Black beans, light & dark red kidney beans: 10 oz., each & rinsed
- Lime juice: 2 tsp.
- 2 minced cloves of garlic
- Olive oil: 1 tbsp.
- 1 butternut squash, chopped
- Medium-firm tofu: 1 lb.
- Canned diced tomatoes: 20 oz., low-sodium
- Chili powder: 2 tbsp.
- Salt & pepper, to taste
- Chipotle powder: half tbsp.

Directions

1. Sauté squash, peppers, onion and garlic in hot oil. Cover the pot and cook for ten minutes on medium-low flame. Stirring as needed.
2. Add the rest of the ingredients, stir well. Cook, covered for 20 minutes on low flame.
3. Mash with a masher to a chunkier consistency. Serve.

Nutrition Per Serving: Kcal 270 | Sodium 201 mg | Protein 31 g | Carbs 45 g | Fat 2 g | Potassium: 301 mg

25. Power Chicken Salad

Preparation time: 20 minutes | Cooking time: 0 minutes | Serving: 4

Ingredients

- Light mayo & Dijon mustard: 1 tbsp., each
- Shelled edamame: half cup, cooked
- Garlic powder & Herbs de Provence: ¼ tsp., each
- Greek yogurt: ¼ cup
- Salt & pepper, to taste
- Half red onion, chopped
- Canned chicken breast: 6 oz.

Directions

1. Add all the ingredients to a bowl, mix well and serve chilled with crackers.

Nutrition Per Serving: Kcal 150 | Sodium 253 mg | Protein 18 g | Carbs 5 g | Fat 6 g | Potassium: 301 mg

26. Parmesan & Roasted Fauxtatoe

Preparation time: 20 minutes | Cooking time: 30 minutes | Serving: 4-6

Ingredients

- Canned Cannellini Beans: 10 oz., rinsed
- Water: 1 cup
- Salt, to taste
- Chicken broth: 1 cup, low-sodium
- White pepper: half tsp.
- 2 cloves garlic
- Cauliflower florets: 3 cups
- Parmesan cheese: half cup, low-fat

Directions:

1. Let the oven preheat to 350 F.
2. Add water, broth and peeled garlic cloves to a pot. Let it come to a boil, add florets.
3. Cook, covered for 5 to 7 minutes.
4. Take the garlic out with half of the liquid, add cheese and beans.
5. Puree with a stick blender. Transfer to a baking dish, bake for 20 to 25 minutes at 350 F.

6. Serve.

Nutrition Per Serving: Kcal 83| Sodium 257 mg | Protein 7 g | Carbs 10 g | Fat 6 g | Potassium: 208 mg

27. Taco Casserole

Preparation time: 20 minutes | Cooking time: 30 minutes | Serving: 9

Ingredients

- 1 zucchini, chopped
- 1 sweet onion, chopped
- Taco seasoning: 1 pack
- Ground turkey: 1 lb.
- Tomatoes & chiles: 8 oz., canned
- Canned refried beans: 8 oz., non-fat
- Mexican cheese blend: 2 cups, low-fat
- 1 minced garlic clove
- Black beans: 10 oz., rinsed

Directions

1. Let the oven preheat to 350 F.
2. Oil spray a hot pan and sauté garlic and vegetables till tender. Drain any liquid and place in a bowl.
3. Cook the meat, drain and place in the bowl.
4. Add taco seasoning, chilies and tomatoes, mix well. Place in a casserole dish (13 by 9).
5. Spread the beans on top. Add cheese.
6. Bake for half an hour at 350 F. Cool slightly, and serve.

Nutrition Per Serving: Kcal 208| Sodium 302 mg | Protein 21 g | Carbs 8 g | Fat 8 g | Potassium: 113 mg

28. Skinny Meatloaf Muffins

Preparation time: 20 minutes | Cooking time: 40 minutes | Serving: 9

Ingredients

- Worcestershire sauce: 2 tbsp.
- Low-carb bread crumbs: half cup
- Diced onion: 1 cup
- Lean ground turkey breast: 1.25 pounds
- Salt & pepper, to taste
- 1 egg
- BBQ sauce: half cup, no-sugar-added

Toppings

- BBQ sauce: 1/3 cup, no-sugar-added

Directions

1. Let the oven preheat to 350 F. Oil spray 9 muffin cups.
2. In a bowl, add all ingredients and mix with clean hands.
3. Spoon into prepared muffin cups and brush with the BBQ sauce.
4. Bake for 40 minutes. Cool slightly, serve.

Nutrition Per Serving: Kcal 115| Sodium 317 mg | Protein 18 g | Carbs 8 g | Fat 1.6 g | Potassium: 273 mg

29. Spicy Summer Beans & Sausage

Preparation time: 20 minutes | Cooking time: 8 hours | Serving: 6

Ingredients

- 1 sweet onion, chopped
- Northern beans dry: 1 lb.
- 2 tomatoes, diced without seeds
- Kosher salt, to taste
- Andouille sausage: 8 oz., diced
- 3 minced garlic cloves
- 1 diced jalapeno pepper, without seeds
- Cajun spice blend: 2 tsp.
- Chicken broth: 4 cups
- Smoked paprika: 1 tsp.
- Water: 2 cups

Directions

1. Oil spray a hot pan and cook sausage until browned.
2. Add tomatoes and onion, cook for 2 minutes.
3. Add garlic and cook for 1 minute. Transfer to a crockpot.
4. Add the rest of the ingredients. Stir well.
5. Cook for 8 hours on low, mash with a stick blender to a chunkier consistency. Serve.

Nutrition Per Serving: Kcal 275| Sodium 337 mg | Protein 21 g | Carbs 15 g | Fat 5 g | Potassium: 312 mg

30. Strawberry Oatmeal Bars

Preparation time: 20 minutes | Cooking time: 45 minutes | Serving: 16

Ingredients

- Whole-wheat flour: ¾ cup
- Ground ginger: half tsp.
- Light brown sugar substitute: 1/3 cup
- Salt: ¼ tsp.
- Ground cinnamon: half tsp.
- Granulated sugar substitute: 1 tbsp.
- Old-fashioned rolled oats: 1 cup
- Lemon juice: 1 tbsp
- Melted butter: 6 tbsp.
- Cornstarch: 1 tsp.
- Vanilla: 1 tsp.
- Diced strawberries: 2 cups

Directions

1. Let the oven preheat to 375 F. Take an 8 by 8 baking pan, line with parchment paper, and oil spray the lined pan.
2. In a bowl, mix vanilla and butter.
3. In a different bowl, toss strawberries, sugar, lemon juice and cornstarch.
4. Add the rest of the ingredients to a third bowl and mix.
5. Add the butter mixture to the third bowl and mix until clumpy.
6. In the prepared pan, add half of the oats mixture, spread the strawberries mixture on top.
7. Add the rest of the oats mixture on top. Bake for 35 to 40 minutes.
8. Cool, slice & serve.

Nutrition Per Serving: Kcal 269 | Sodium 117 mg | Protein 16.3 g | Carbs 9 g | Fat 3.9 g | Potassium: 176 mg

31. Pina Colada Protein Shake

Preparation time: 10 minutes | Cooking time: 0 minutes | Serving: 2

Ingredients

- Plain protein powder: 2 scoops
- Lime juice: 2 tsp.
- Ice: ¼ cup
- Frozen pineapple: 1 cup
- Coconut extract: half tsp.
- Coconut milk: 4 oz.
- Honey: 1 tsp.

Directions

1. Add all ingredients to a blender.
2. Pulse until smooth, serve.

Nutrition Per Serving: Kcal 198 | Sodium 89 mg | Protein 12 g | Carbs 4.5 g | Fat 3 g | Potassium: 166 mg

32. Best High-Protein Soup

Preparation time: 10 minutes | Cooking time: 20 minutes | Serving: 4

Ingredients

- Kosher salt: 1 tsp.
- Olive oil: 1 tbsp.
- Half rotisserie chicken
- Vegetable broth: 3 cups
- Onion, carrot & celery: each diced half cup
- Fresh herbs: ¼ cup, chopped
- Chicken broth: 2 cups
- Cooked brown rice: 1 cup

Directions

1. Shred the chicken and use only half of it; discard the bones.
2. In a pot, saute vegetables in hot oil for 5 minutes.
3. Add broths and salt, let it come to a boil, turn the heat low and simmer for 10 minutes.
4. Add rest of the ingredients, cook for 5 minutes.
5. Serve.

Nutrition Per Serving: Kcal 225 | Sodium 191 mg | Protein 15 g | Carbs 18 g | Fat 10 g | Potassium: 208 mg

33. Breakfast Bowls

Preparation time: 15 minutes | Cooking time: 0 minutes | Serving: 1

Ingredients

- Black beans: 2 tbsp.
- Cooked spinach: 2 tbsp.
- 2 cooked eggs, scrambled
- Salsa: 1 to 2 tbsp.
- Low-fat cheddar cheese: 1 tbsp., shredded

Directions

1. In a jar, layer all the ingredients, keep eggs in the middle.
2. Serve as it is or heat in a bowl.

Nutrition Per Serving: Kcal 210 | Sodium 403 mg | Protein 16.5 g | Carbs 7 g | Fat 12.5 g | Potassium: 318 mg

34. Pumpkin Spice Hot Chocolate

Preparation time: 10 minutes | Cooking time: 0 minutes | Serving: 1

Ingredients

- Hot water: 1 cup
- Hot Chocolate Mix: 1 pack, sugar-free
- Pumpkin spice: half tsp.

Directions

1. In a jug, add all ingredients. Stir well and serve.

Nutrition Per Serving: Kcal 83 | Sodium 220 mg | Protein 15 g | Carbs 4 g | Fat 1 g | Potassium: 209 mg

35. Chicken & Peanut Stew

Preparation time: 10 minutes | Cooking time: 5 hours | Serving: 8

Ingredients

- Peanut butter: 3 tbsp., creamy
- Ground ginger: half tsp.
- Baby spinach: 1 cup
- Cumin: 1 tsp.
- Chicken broth: 1 cup, low-sodium
- Dried coriander: 1 tsp.
- Chickpeas: 1 cup
- Canned diced tomatoes: 1 cup
- Diced chicken breasts: 12 oz., boneless & skinless

Directions

1. Whisk peanut butter, ginger, cumin, broth and coriander, until smooth.
2. Add chickpeas, tomatoes and chicken; coat well. Transfer to a slow cooker.
3. Cook on high for 4 to 5 hours till chicken is cooked.
4. Shred the chicken and cook for 10 minutes, add spinach. Stir and let it rest until it wilts.
5. Serve.

Nutrition Per Serving: Kcal 169 | Sodium 143 mg | Protein 17.5 g | Carbs 11.5 g | Fat 5.9 g | Potassium: 209 mg

36. Scotch Eggs

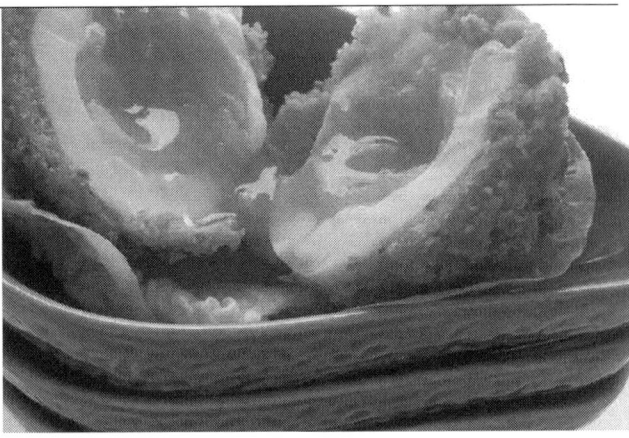

Preparation time: 10 minutes | Cooking time: 20 minutes | Serving: 4

Ingredients

- Low-fat Parmesan cheese: half cup, grated
- 4 hard-boiled eggs
- Italian seasoning & garlic powder: ¼ tsp., each
- Breakfast sausage: 8 oz., ground

Directions

1. Peel and pat dry the eggs.
2. On a surface, make the sausage into a disk and separate it into 4 equal parts. Make each part into a round disk.
3. Place 1 peeled egg on top of the disk and roll the egg in it.
4. In a bowl, add the rest of the ingredients. Toss well.
5. Add coated eggs and roll in the mixture. Oil spray the eggs and bake for 20 minutes at 400 F.
6. Let the eggs cool, then take them off the tray. Serve.

Nutrition Per Serving: Kcal 109 | Sodium 99.9 mg | Protein 21 g | Carbs 8 g | Fat 5 g | Potassium: 117 mg

37. High Protein Egg Salad

Preparation time: 15 minutes | Cooking time: 0 minutes | Serving: 5

Ingredients

- Salt, to taste
- Hard-boiled 5 eggs
- Mustard: 1/8 tsp.
- Cottage cheese: 1/3 cup, low-fat
- Onion powder: 1 tsp.

Directions

1. Roughly chop the eggs and mix with the rest of the ingredients.

2. Pulse in a food processor till soft.
3. Serve.

Nutrition Per Serving: Kcal 210 | Sodium 294 mg | Protein 19 g | Carbs 2.8 g | Fat 12.7 g | Potassium: 216 mg

38. Smoked Salmon Pate

Preparation time: 10 minutes | Cooking time: 0 minutes | Serving: 2

Ingredients

- Greek yogurt: 8 tbsp., low-fat
- Salt & pepper, to taste
- Dried dill: 2 tsp.
- Smoked salmon: 10 oz.
- Lemon juice: 4 tbsp.

Directions

1. In a food processor, add all ingredients, except for yogurt. Pulse until smooth.
2. Mix in the yogurt and serve.

Nutrition Per Serving: Kcal 45 | Sodium 345 mg | Protein 7 g | Carbs 1 g | Fat 2 g | Potassium: 101 mg

39. Crustless Quiche

Preparation time: 10 minutes | Cooking time: 30 minutes | Serving: 4

Ingredients

- Skim milk: 1 cup
- Cooked Mushroom & spinach: half cup, each
- Low-fat cheese: half cup
- 6 eggs
- Butter: 4 tbsp.

Directions

1. In a bowl, whisk eggs, milk, butter and cheese.
2. Add vegetables and pour into a baking dish.
3. Bake for 25 to 30 minutes at 375 F.
4. Slice and serve.

Nutrition Per Serving: Kcal 120 | Sodium 128 mg | Protein 12 g | Carbs 4 g | Fat 2.2 g | Potassium: 118 mg

40. Peanut Butter Protein Bars

Preparation time: 70 minutes | Cooking time: 5 minutes | Serving: 12

Ingredients

- Liquid no-calorie Sweetener: 1/3 cup
- Mini chocolate chips: 1/3 cup, sugar-free
- Coconut oil: 2 tbsp.
- Flaxseed meal: 3 tbsp.
- Creamy peanut butter: ¾ cup
- Kosher salt: ¼ tsp.
- Rolled Oats: 2 cups
- Protein vanilla powder: half cup
- Ground cinnamon: ¼ tsp.

Directions

1. Take an 8 by 8 baking pan and line it with parchment paper; let it hang on the sides.
2. In a bowl, add oil, peanut butter and sweetener. Place the bowl on simmering water and whisk until combined.
3. Add the rest of the ingredients to a food processor and pulse until smooth.
4. Take the bowl off the water and add the rest of the ingredients, except for chocolate chips.
5. If it is hot, let it cool for few minutes, then add chocolate chips.
6. Place in the prepared pan and press. Keep in the fridge for 60 minutes.
7. Slice and serve.

Nutrition Per Serving: Kcal 244 | Sodium 128 mg | Protein 9 g | Carbs 26 g | Fat 14 g | Potassium: 118 mg

41. Swede Soup

Preparation time: 10 minutes | Cooking time: 230 minutes | Serving: 3-4

Ingredients

- 2 carrots, chopped
- 1 onion, chopped
- Thyme & paprika: half tsp., each

- 1 minced garlic clove
- Roasted swede: 2 cups
- Chicken stock: 4 cups
- Ground nutmeg: ¼ tsp.
- Salt & pepper, to taste

Directions

1. In a pan, saute onion in hot oil until tender.
2. Add garlic and cook for 60 seconds. Add the rest of the ingredients, cook until tender.
3. Puree with a stick blender, adjust seasoning and serve.

Nutrition Per Serving: Kcal 54 | Sodium 325 mg | Protein 1 g | Carbs 12 g | Fat 1 g | Potassium: 351 mg

42. Chili Lime Turkey Burgers

Preparation time: 10 minutes | Cooking time: 10 minutes | Serving: 4

Ingredients

- Ground turkey: 1 lb.
- 1 lime's juice & zest
- Chopped red bell pepper: ¼ cup
- Chili powder: 1 tsp.
- Cilantro: 2 tbsp., chopped
- Greek yogurt: ¼ cup, low-fat
- Olive oil: 1 tbsp.

Directions

1. Add all ingredients, except for oil, to a bowl. Mix and make into 4 patties.
2. In a pan, heat oil on medium flame. Cook patties for 4 to 5 minutes on each side.
3. Serve.

Nutrition Per Serving: Kcal 144.7 | Sodium 65 mg | Protein 25 g | Carbs 1.5 g | Fat 4.5 g | Potassium: 281 mg

43. Shakshuka

Preparation time: 10 minutes | Cooking time: 20 minutes | Serving: 4

Ingredients

- Olive oil: 1 tbsp.
- Paprika: 2 tsp.
- Canned tomatoes: 20 oz.
- 1 onion, sliced thin
- 2 minced garlic cloves
- 1 bunch of parsley
- Salt & pepper, to taste
- 4 eggs
- Cumin: half tsp.
- Chili powder: ¼ tsp.

Directions

1. Saute onion in hot oil for 2 minutes.
2. Add garlic and cook for 1 minute more; add tomatoes and spices. Cook for few minutes.
3. Break eggs on top of the tomatoes. Turn the heat low and cook for 5 to 8 minutes, covered.
4. Let it cool slightly and serve.

Nutrition Per Serving: Kcal 201 | Sodium 141 mg | Protein 15.9 g | Carbs 2 g | Fat 3.4 g | Potassium: 301 mg

44. Spanakopita Chicken Patties

Preparation time: 10 minutes | Cooking time: 20 minutes | Serving: 8

Ingredients

- Lean ground chicken: 16 oz.
- Dried oregano: half tsp.
- 1 egg
- 2 minced garlic cloves
- Canned chickpeas: half cup, rinsed
- Feta cheese: 2 oz., low-fat
- Parsley: 1 tbsp., chopped
- Spinach: 1 cup, sliced
- Paprika: half tsp.

Directions

1. Let the oven preheat to 350 F, oil spray a baking sheet.
2. Process the chickpeas in a food processor until crumbly.
3. In a bowl, add chickpeas with the rest of the ingredients. Mix until combined.
4. Make into 8 patties and bake for 18 to 20 minutes on the baking sheet.
5. Serve.

Nutrition Per Serving: Kcal 112.1 | Sodium 163 mg | Protein 13.9 g | Carbs 0.8 g | Fat 6.1 g | Potassium: 301 mg

45. Cranberry Chicken Salad

Preparation time: 15 minutes | Cooking time: 0 minutes | Serving: 8

Ingredients

- Cottage cheese: ¼ cup, low-fat
- Chopped parsley: 2 tbsp.
- Boiled chicken breasts (boneless & skinless): 2 cups, shredded
- Chopped dill: 2 tbsp.
- Celery: ¼ cup, chopped
- Greek yogurt: ¼ tbsp., low-fat
- Carrots: ¼ cup, shredded
- Lemon juice: 1 tbsp.
- Fresh cranberries: ¼ cup, chopped

Directions

1. Mix yogurt, cheese with lemon juice in a bowl.
2. Add the rest of the ingredients, mix well and serve.

Nutrition Per Serving: Kcal 92 | Sodium 112 mg | Protein 17 g | Carbs 1 g | Fat 2 g | Potassium: 302 mg

46. Spinach & Mushroom Egg Cups

Preparation time: 10 minutes | Cooking time: 20 minutes | Serving: 4

Ingredients

- Spinach: 2 oz., chopped
- Greek yogurt: 3 tbsp.
- 12 eggs
- Shredded cheddar: half cup, low-fat
- Mushrooms: 3 oz., chopped

Directions

1. Let the oven preheat to 350 F. oil spray a muffin tin.
2. Take 8 eggs and separate the yolks, discard them add the whites with the rest of the eggs.
3. Whisk with yogurt. Add the rest of the ingredients and mix.
4. Pour into the muffin tin (8 cups), bake for 22 to 25 minutes.

Nutrition Per Serving: Kcal 119 | Sodium 182 mg | Protein 12.6 g | Carbs 2.1 g | Fat 6.5 g | Potassium: 265 mg

47. Italian Meatloaf

Preparation time: 10 minutes | Cooking time: 45 minutes | Serving: 8

Ingredients

- Diced zucchini: half cup
- Almond flour: ¼ cup
- Red onions: ¼ cup, chopped
- Ground lean beef: 16 oz.
- Grated parmesan: 2 tbsp.
- 1 egg
- 2 minced cloves of garlic
- Diced tomatoes: ¾ cup
- Ground turkey: 8 oz.
- Italian seasoning: 1 tsp., unsalted

Directions

1. Let the oven preheat to 400 F.
2. Sauté onion with water (2 tbsp.) for 3 to 4 minutes.
3. Add zucchini and sauté for 3 to 4 minutes. Add garlic and sauté for half a second.
4. Take it out in a bowl. Cool slightly and add the rest of the ingredients, except for tomatoes.
5. Mix until combined, transfer to a parchment-lined loaf pan.
6. Add crushed tomatoes on top. Bake for 30 to 40 minutes.
7. Serve.

Nutrition Per Serving: Kcal 175 | Sodium 94 mg | Protein 26.3 g | Carbs 3.5 g | Fat 6.2 g | Potassium: 265 mg

48. Creamy Tuscan Shrimp

Preparation time: 10 minutes | Cooking time: 20 minutes | Serving: 8

Ingredients

- Shrimp: 8 oz., peeled & deveined
- 3 minced cloves of garlic
- Greek yogurt: 3 tbsp., low-fat
- Baby arugula: 2 cups
- Unsalted butter: 1 tsp.
- Parsley: 2 tbsp., chopped
- Diced tomatoes: ¾ cup
- Italian seasoning: 1 tsp., unsalted

Directions

1. In a pan, add melt on medium flame. Add shrimps and cook for 1 to 2 minutes.
2. Add garlic and sauté for 1 minute.
3. Add arugula and cook until it wilts.
4. Add the rest of the ingredients, cook for 2-3 minutes.
5. Pulse into a chunky mixture and serve.

Nutrition Per Serving: Kcal 55| Sodium 50.7 mg | Protein 6.8 g | Carbs 2.2 g | Fat 2.1 g | Potassium: 217 mg

49. Cheesy Chicken & Broccoli Casserole

Preparation time: 10 minutes| Cooking time: 25 minutes| Serving: 8

Ingredients

- Red bell pepper: 1 cup, sliced
- Olive oil: half tbsp.
- Cooked chicken breasts (boneless & skinless): 2 cups, shredded
- Cilantro: 2 tbsp., chopped
- Greek yogurt: ¼ cup, low-fat
- 1 egg
- Broccoli florets: 2 cups, chopped
- Cheddar cheese: half cup, low-fat

Directions

1. Let the oven preheat to 400 F. oil spray a small casserole dish.
2. Sauté bell pepper in hot oil for 4 minutes.
3. Add florets and cook for 1 to 2 minutes. Turn the heat and cool slightly.
4. In a bowl, whisk the egg with yogurt. Add cheese and mix.
5. Add pepper mixture with chicken. Mix well.
6. Spoon into the dish and spread. Bake for 20 to 25 minutes.
7. Serve.

Nutrition Per Serving: Kcal 189| Sodium 106 mg | Protein 2 g | Carbs 2.5 g | Fat 7.2 g | Potassium: 301 mg

50. Cauliflower "Fried Rice"

Preparation time: 10 minutes| Cooking time: 20 minutes| Serving: 4

Ingredients

- Diced bell pepper: ¼ cup
- Riced cauliflower: 8 oz.
- Diced carrots: ¼ cup
- Peas: 2 tbsp.
- 4 egg whites
- Sesame oil: 1 tsp.
- Chopped bok choy: half cup
- Soy sauce: 1 ½ tbsp., low-sodium
- Cilantro: 2 tbsp., chopped
- Rice vinegar: half tbsp.

Directions

1. Cook eggs in a splash of water and take them out in a bowl.
2. Sauté peppers in hot oil for 3 to 4 minutes. Add bok choy and cook for 2 to 3 minutes.
3. Whisk vinegar, water (2 tbsp.) and soy sauce.
4. In the skillet, add cauliflower rice with vegetables and the soy sauce mixture.
5. Cook for 4 to 5 minutes, covered. Add peas and cook for 2 to 3 minutes.
6. Add eggs and toss, serve.

Nutrition Per Serving: Kcal 68| Sodium 535 mg | Protein 6 g | Carbs 4.7 g | Fat 2.4 g | Potassium: 307 mg

51. Bacon & Vegetable Soup

Preparation time: 10 minutes| Cooking time: 25 minutes| Serving: 6

Ingredients

- 1 onion, quartered
- Bacon: 2 oz., chopped
- Tomato paste: 5 oz.
- Chopped mix vegetables: 17 oz.
- Stock concentrate: 2 tbsp.
- 2 garlic cloves
- Water: 35.3 oz.
- Black pepper, to taste

Directions

1. In a food processor, add vegetables and chop roughly. Take it out in a bowl.
2. Chop the garlic and onion roughly. Add to a pot with bacon and oil. Cook for 5 minutes.
3. Add the rest of the ingredients. Cook for 15 minutes. Serve.

Nutrition Per Serving: Kcal 125| Sodium 501 mg | Protein 7.6 g | Carbs 4 g | Fat 2.4 g | Potassium: 307 mg

52. Great Northern Beans and Sausage

Preparation time: 12 minutes | Cooking time: 6-8 hours | Serving: 5-6

Ingredients

- Smoked paprika: 1 ½ tsp.
- 1 sweet onion, chopped
- 1 lb. Northern dry beans
- Water: 2 cups
- 2 small tomatoes, diced without seeds
- 2 garlic cloves, minced
- Cajun spice blend: 1 ½ tsp.
- Chicken broth: 4 cups
- Pork sausage: 8 oz., diced small
- Salt: half tsp.
- 1 jalapeno pepper, diced

Directions

1. Add sausage to a non-stick pan and cook until browned.
2. Add onions, tomato and cook for 2 minutes.
3. Add garlic and cook for 2 minutes more. Transfer to a crockpot with the rest of the ingredients, mix well.
4. Let it cook for 6-8 hours on low.
5. Serve.

Nutrition Per Serving: Kcal 275 | Sodium 476 mg | Protein 21 g | Carbs 12 g | Fat 11 g | Potassium: 359 mg

53. Instant Pot Turkey Chili

Preparation time: 12 minutes | Cooking time: 15 minutes | Serving: 6

Ingredients

- Ground lean turkey: 1 lb.
- 1 onion, diced
- Chicken broth: 1 cup
- 1 can of (28 oz.) Crushed tomato
- Olive oil: 2 tbsp.
- Chili powder: 1 ½ tbsp.
- Kidney beans: 1 can, rinsed
- Cumin: 1 ½ tsp.
- Salt & pepper to taste

Directions

1. In an instant pot, select saute. Heat oil and cook onions until tender.
2. Add turkey and spices, cook until browned.
3. Add broth and tomatoes, stir. Cook for 10 minutes on high.
4. Release the valva, add beans. Pulse into a chunkier consistency.
5. Serve.

Nutrition Per Serving: Kcal 232 | Sodium 337 mg | Protein 19.4 g | Carbs 15 g | Fat 11.4 g | Potassium: 321 mg

54. Chicken Taco Chili

Preparation time: 12 minutes | Cooking time: 6 hours | Serving: 10

Ingredients

- 1 can of (~16 oz.) black beans, drained
- Canned tomatoes w/chilies: 20 oz., diced
- 1 can of (~16 oz.) kidney beans, drained
- 1 onion, chopped
- Corn kernels: 10 oz.
- Chili powder: 1 tbsp.
- Canned green chili peppers: 4 oz., chopped
- Tomato sauce: 8 oz.
- Taco seasoning: 1 pack, low-sodium
- Fresh cilantro: ¼ cup, chopped
- Cumin: 1 tbsp.
- 3 chicken breasts, boneless & skinless

Directions

1. In a slow cooker, add all ingredients except for chicken.
2. Mix well and place chicken; cover it completely.
3. Cook for 8-10 hours on low or 4-6 hours on high.
4. Take the chicken out and shred finely. Put it back in the cooker, mix well.
5. Serve.

Nutrition Per Serving: Kcal 220 | Sodium 729 mg | Protein 21 g | Carbs 28 g | Fat 11.4 g | Potassium: 409 mg

55. Turkey Meatloaf

Preparation time: 12 minutes | Cooking time: 1 hour & 6 minutes | Serving: 8

Ingredients

- Chopped onion: 1 1/2 cups
- Worcestershire sauce: 1 ½ tbsp.
- 2 chopped cloves of garlic
- Dry breadcrumbs: ¾ cup
- 1 egg white, whisked
- Olive oil: 1 tbsp.
- Salt: ¾ tsp.
- Ketchup: 3 tbsp.
- Pepper: half tsp.
- Chicken broth: 1/3 cup
- 1 egg, whisked
- Lean ground turkey: 1 ¾ pound

Directions

1. Let the oven preheat to 375 F.

2. Saute onion in hot oil for 5 minutes. Add garlic, salt & pepper (1/4 tsp. each), cook for 1 minute.
3. Add ketchup (1 tbsp.), broth and Worcestershire sauce. Mix and take it out in a bowl, cool slightly.
4. Add the rest of the ingredients (except for ketchup) to the same bowl. Mix well.
5. Oil spray a foil-lined baking sheet. Place the mixture and make it into a loaf.
6. Brush with ketchup.
7. Bake for 60 minutes until the internal temperature of the loaf reaches 170 F.
8. Slice and serve.

Nutrition Per Serving: Kcal 209| Sodium 356 mg | Protein 25 g | Carbs 13 g | Fat 7 g | Potassium: 356 mg

56. Granola Bar

Preparation time: 3 hours & 10 minutes| Cooking time: 15 minutes| Serving: 16

Ingredients

- 3/4 cup of wheat germ
- 2/3 cup of brown sugar substitute
- 8 oz. of dried fruit
- 3/4 cup of sunflower seeds
- 2 cups of oats
- 2 tsp. of vanilla extract
- Half cup of honey
- Half tsp. of Kosher salt
- 4 Tbsp of butter
- 1 cup of crushed peanuts

Directions

1. Let the oven preheat to 400 F.
2. In a baking dish, add seeds, peanuts, wheat germ and oats, toss well.
3. Toast in the oven for 10 to 12 minutes, shaking the dish to prevent burning.
4. Line a baking dish (11 by 13") with parchment paper.
5. In a pan, add vanilla, sugar, salt, honey and butter and let it simmer, stirring as needed.
6. In a large bowl, add toasted grains with the rest of the ingredients. Mix.
7. Transfer to the prepared dish, spread and add a sheet of parchment on top; press down.
8. Let it rest for 2 to 3 hours. Slice & serve.

Nutrition Per Serving: Kcal 267| Sodium 500 mg | Protein 6 g | Carbs 38 g | Fat 12 g | Potassium: 301 mg

57. Cocoa Almond Protein Smoothie

Preparation time: 10 minutes| Cooking time: 0 minute| Serving: 2

Ingredients

- Skim milk: 2 tbsp. + ¼ cup
- 1 banana
- Greek yogurt: ¾ cup low-fat
- Almond butter: 2 tbsp.
- Ice cubes: ¾ cup
- Cocoa powder: 2 tbsp., unsweetened
- Ground flaxseed: 2 tsp.

Directions

1. Add all the ingredients to a blender.
2. Pulse until smooth, serve.

Nutrition Per Serving: Kcal 255| Sodium 201 mg | Protein 4.3 g | Carbs 3.3 g | Fat 3.2 g | Potassium: 287 mg

58. Hashbrown Egg Casserole

Preparation time: 10 minutes| Cooking time: 80 minutes| Serving: 12

Ingredients

- Turkey sausage: 1 lb.
- 1 diced onion
- Shredded hash browns: 20 oz., thawed
- 1 chopped red bell pepper
- Italian seasoning: half tsp.
- Baby spinach: 2 cups, sliced
- 12 eggs
- Shredded cheddar cheese: half cup, low-fat
- Skim milk: 1 ¼ cups
- Salt: 1 tsp.
- Black pepper: ¼ tsp.

Directions

1. Let the oven preheat to 350 F. Oil spray a 9 by 13" baking dish.
2. In a pan, cook sausage with onion until browned. Add spinach, mix and let it cool.
3. Add the rest of the ingredients (except for hash brown & cheese) to a bowl and whisk, add hash brown and sausage mixture. Mix and transfer to the baking dish.
4. Top with shredded cheese. Bake for 70 minutes.
5. Slice and serve.

Nutrition Per Serving: Kcal 287| Sodium 289 mg | Protein 21 g | Carbs 17.8 g | Fat 4.9 g | Potassium: 309 mg

59. Lemon Garlic Salmon Baked

Preparation time: 10 minutes| Cooking time: 20 minutes| Serving: 4

Ingredients

- Black pepper, to taste
- Olive oil: 1 tbsp.
- 3 minced garlic cloves
- Salt: ¼ tsp.
- Salmon fillet: 1 ½ pound
- Butter diced: 2 tbsp.
- Half lemon's juice
- Italian seasoning: 1 tsp., salt-free

Directions

1. Let the oven preheat to 400 F. oil spray a foil-lined baking sheet.
2. Place fish on top and coat with oil, and spread garlic on top.
3. Pour lemon juice on top, season with salt, pepper and Italian seasoning.
4. Place butter on top, wrap in foil.
5. Bake for 10 to 15 minutes.

Nutrition Per Serving: Kcal 328| Sodium 267 mg | Protein 34 g | Carbs 1 g | Fat 20 g | Potassium: 311 mg

60. Lentil, Haricot Bean & Chickpea Soup

Preparation time: 10 minutes| Cooking time: 20 minutes| Serving: 4

Ingredients

- 1 red onion, diced
- 3 minced garlic cloves
- Olive oil: 2 tbsp.
- Canned chopped tomatoes: 14 oz.
- Half red & green pepper, each chopped
- Chicken stock: 28 oz.
- Chickpeas: 7 oz.
- Red split lentils: 5 oz.
- Haricot beans: 3.5 oz.
- 1 lemon's juice
- Salt & pepper

Directions

1. Saute garlic and onion in hot oil. Transfer to a pot.
2. Add the rest of the ingredients and let it come to a boil.
3. Simmer on low for 20 minutes. Add more broth if needed.
4. Adjust seasoning and serve.

Nutrition Per Serving: Kcal 208| Sodium 178 mg | Protein 8.9 g | Carbs 4 g | Fat 8 g | Potassium: 311 mg

Chapter 7: Stage 4: General Phase

This stage begins 4 to 6 weeks following your operation and entails the reintroduction of normal meals! Begin by introducing 1 to 2 new meals each day while avoiding foods that induce gas, such as pepper, spicy foods, onions, broccoli. Remember to chew thoroughly before swallowing and to eat gradually.

- Rice, bread & pasta
- Alcohol
- Dry meats
- Thick-skinned fruit
- Fried meals
- Carbonated drinks
- Added sweets

Each meal should be approximately a 1/3 cup (6 oz.) and not more than one cup. Continue to follow the 30/30 guideline by drinking water between those meals. You will soon be able to return to a normal diet. However, there are still certain items you should avoid:

- Baked products
- Oils

Three-four meals each day are sufficient. Eat until you are satisfied, or until you've consumed a cup of food, and then quit. Wait till the next meal to consume anything solid, blended, or soft.

- Fish, skinless & boneless chicken, and turkey are the finest meals to consume. These contain a lot of protein.
- It's ideal if you stay away from grains, potatoes, and bread. Continue to consume protein-rich foods while avoiding carbs and fats.
- Limit your intake of high-fat sauces such as mayonnaise or butter. Other condiments are OK. However, excessive ketchup consumption may induce dumping syndrome due to its high sugar level.
- Don't ever drink anything other than water with the meals.
- Keep drinking 48 64 ounces of liquids each day, but only in between meals.
- Avoid eating two to three hours before bedtime.

Part 1: Appetizers, Snacks & Sides

1. Mozzarella sticks

Preparation time: 15 minutes | Cooking time: 10 minutes | Serving: 6

Ingredients

- Bread crumbs: 2 tbsp., whole-wheat
- Grated parmesan cheese: 2 tbsp., low-fat
- High fiber cereal: half cup, crushed
- 3 mozzarella string cheese, part-skim, halved
- Onion powder: ¼ tsp.
- Italian seasoning: 1/8 tsp., salt-free
- 1 egg, whisked
- Salt & black pepper, to taste
- Water: 1 tbsp.

Directions

1. Let the oven preheat to 350 F.
2. In a bowl, whisk the egg with water.
3. In a different bowl, mix spices, cereal, parmesan and crumbs.
4. Coat the cheese strings in egg then in cereal mixture. Repeat the process if needed.
5. Bake for ten minutes on parchment-lined baking paper.
6. Serve with marinara sauce.

Nutrition Per Serving: Kcal 211 | Sodium 167 mg | Protein 11.1 g | Carbs 13 g | Fat 10 g | Potassium: 309 mg

2. Avocado Mango Mash

Preparation time: 15 minutes | Cooking time: 0 minutes | Serving: 4

Ingredients

- 2 minced garlic cloves
- 3 avocados, cubed
- Half jalapeno, chopped without seeds
- 1 mango, cubed
- Ground cumin: 1 tsp.
- Sliced green onion: ¼ cup
- Sea salt & black pepper: ¼ tsp., each
- Cayenne pepper, to taste
- 1 lime's juice
- Fresh cilantro: 2 tbsp., chopped

Directions

1. Add all ingredients to a bowl, mash to your desired consistency.
2. Serve.

Nutrition Per Serving: Kcal 256 | Sodium 201 mg | Protein 18 g | Carbs 4.5 g | Fat 13.4 g | Potassium: 301 mg

3. Protein Strawberry Cheesecake Cheeseball

Preparation time: 3 hours & 10 minutes | Cooking time: 0 minutes | Serving: 8

Ingredients

- No-calorie sweetener: ¾ cup
- Strawberry jelly: half cup, sugar-free
- Vanilla extract: half tbsp.
- Greek yogurt cream cheese: 16 oz., low-fat
- High fiber cereal: 2 cups
- Protein powder: 3 servings
- Diced strawberries: 2 cups

Directions

1. In a bowl, add cream cheese and beat with protein powder, vanilla and sweetener.
2. Drain the jelly and add to the cream cheese mixture with strawberries.
3. Fold it in. Transfer to a plastic wrap and make into a ball. Keep in the fridge for 3 hours.
4. Serve with graham crackers.

Nutrition Per Serving: Kcal 278 | Sodium 276 mg | Protein 13 g | Carbs 5 g | Fat 11.3 g | Potassium: 276 mg

4. Zucchini Artichoke Bites

Preparation time: 10 minutes | Cooking time: 20 minutes | Serving: 6

Ingredients

- Shredded parmesan cheese: 3 oz., low-fat
- Greek yogurt: half cup, non-fat
- Canned artichoke hearts: 1 & ½ can, diced without liquid
- Greek seasoning: 1 ½ tbsp.
- 1 1/2 red bell pepper, chopped
- 1 1/2 minced clove garlic
- 3 zucchini, sliced rounds

Directions

1. Let the oven preheat to 425 F. Line a baking sheet with parchment paper and place zucchini slices on top.
2. Add the rest of the ingredients to a bowl and mix well.
3. Spoon the mixture onto zucchini slices. Bake for 14 to 16 minutes.
4. Cool & serve.

Nutrition Per 2 oz.: Kcal 53 | Sodium 454 mg | Protein 5 g | Carbs 5 g | Fat 2 g | Potassium: 409 mg

5. Stuffed Mushrooms

Preparation time: 15 minutes | Cooking time: 10 minutes | Serving: 4

Ingredients

- 8 mushrooms, medium-sized
- Beef Bouillon Soup: 1 pack, low-sodium
- Swiss cheese: 2 oz., low-fat, grated

Directions

1. Let the oven preheat to 400 F.
2. Break the mushroom's stems and chop them. Mix the chopped stems with cheese.
3. Take the mushrooms out of the cap, leaving a shell.
4. Spoon the mixture into each shell. Sprinkle water and beef soup on top.
5. Bake 5-10 minutes, serve.

Nutrition Per Serving: Kcal 102 | Sodium 171 mg | Protein 18 g | Carbs 4 g | Fat 2 g | Potassium: 354 mg

6. Pumpkin Spice Chia Seed Pudding

Preparation time: 10 minutes | Cooking time: 0 minutes | Serving: 4

Ingredients

- Pumpkin pie spice: 2 tsp.
- Canned coconut milk: ¾ cup
- Liquid stevia: 1 tsp.
- Pumpkin puree: half cup
- Skim milk: ¾ cup
- Chia seeds: half cup

Directions

1. Add all ingredients to a bowl, and mix well.
2. Transfer to serving dishes, serve chilled.

Nutrition Per Serving.: Kcal 117 | Sodium 78 mg | Protein 13 g | Carbs 6 g | Fat 1.2 g | Potassium: 209 mg

7. Instant Chicken Gravy

Preparation time: 10 minutes | Cooking time: 0 minutes | Serving: 4

Ingredients

- warm water: half cup
- Cream of Chicken Soup: 1 pack, low-sodium

Directions

1. Add all ingredients to a bowl, mix well. Serve.

Nutrition Per Serving.: Kcal 95 | Sodium 78 mg | Protein 20 g | Carbs 12 g | Fat 2 g | Potassium: 209 mg

8. Caprese Snack Bowl

Preparation time: 10 minutes | Cooking time: 0 minutes | Serving: 4

Ingredients

- 10 to 12 cherry tomatoes, halved
- Balsamic glaze: 1 tsp.
- Sea salt & black pepper: ¼ tsp., each
- Fresh basil: 1 tsp., sliced
- Light mozzarella: 2 sticks, cut into one" pieces

- Olive oil: 1 tsp.

Directions

2. In a bowl, mix basil, tomatoes and cheese.
3. Add glaze and oil, toss to coat. Serve

Nutrition Per Serving.: Kcal 78 | Sodium 93 mg | Protein 11 g | Carbs 2 g | Fat 4 g | Potassium: 211 mg

9. Chicken Salad Cucumber Bites

Preparation time: 15 minutes | Cooking time: 0 minutes | Serving: 4

Ingredients

- Half cucumber, sliced into circles
- Red onion: 1/3 cup, diced
- Light Mayonaise: 1/3 cup
- 1 chicken breast, cooked & diced
- Salt & pepper, to taste

Directions

1. In a bowl, add all ingredients except for cucumber slices.
2. Mix and spoon onto cucumber slices, serve.

Nutrition Per Serving: Kcal 55 | Sodium 67 mg | Protein 21 g | Carbs 3 g | Fat 2 g | Potassium: 201 mg

10. Zucchini Chips

Preparation time: 10 minutes | Cooking time: 10 minutes | Serving: 4

Ingredients

- One large zucchini
- Kosher salt, to taste
- Olive oil: 2 tbsp.

Directions

1. Let the oven preheat to 225 F.
2. Line 2 baking sheets with parchment paper. Thinly slice the zucchini and place it on paper towels, and pat dry.
3. Spread the slices onto the baking sheet in 1 even layer.
4. Brush with olive oil and sprinkle with salt.
5. Bake for 2 hours. Let them cool and serve.

Nutrition Per Serving: Kcal 45 | Sodium 109 mg | Protein 2 g | Carbs 1 g | Fat 2 g | Potassium: 202 mg

11. Mock Mashed Potatoes

Preparation time: 10 minutes | Cooking time: 10 minutes | Serving: 4

Ingredients

- Frozen cauliflower: 8 oz.
- Chicken Bouillon Soup: 1 pack, low-sodium

Directions

1. Cook cauliflower as you like, until tender. Mash and mix with half of the soup pack.
2. Mix and serve.

Nutrition Per Serving: Kcal 87 | Sodium 109 mg | Protein 12 g | Carbs 10 g | Fat 1.1 g | Potassium: 202 mg

12. Soft Pretzels

Preparation time: 10 minutes | Cooking time: 10 minutes | Serving: 8

Ingredients

- Warm water: 2 tbsp.
- 1 egg, whisked
- Almond flour: 1 cup
- Mozzarella cheese: 1 ½ cups, low-fat
- Melted butter: 1 tbsp.
- Psyllium husk powder: 1 tsp.
- Instant yeast: 1 tsp.
- Baking powder: 1 tsp.
- Kosher salt: half tsp.
- Cream cheese: 1 oz.

Directions

1. Let the oven preheat to 425 F.
2. In a bowl, add yeast and warm water, stir well. Let it rest for 5 to 10 minutes.
3. In a bowl, add all dry ingredients and mix.
4. In a bowl, add cream cheese and mozzarella, microwave for 1 minute and mix, microwave again until melted.
5. Add the yeast to the cheese mixture.
6. Add egg and then the dry ingredients, mix with oil sprayed hands, till a dough forms.
7. Cut into 4 pieces, roll each piece into four" long, and then cut into 4 pieces. Shape into a pretzel

8. Place on a parchment lined baking sheet. Bake for 10 minutes.
9. Brush with melted butter, add salt on top. Serve.

Nutrition Per 2 pretzel: Kcal 171 | Sodium 296 mg | Protein 9 g | Carbs 4 g | Fat 13 g | Potassium: 94 mg

13. Angelic Chicken

Preparation time: 10 minutes | Cooking time: 0 minutes | Serving: 2-3

Ingredients

- Onion salt, black pepper & garlic powder, to taste
- Non-fat Greek yogurt: 3 tbsp.
- 3-5 cherry tomatoes, cut into fours
- Light mayo: 2 tbsp.
- Chicken breast: 1 small can
- Diced onion: 1 tbsp.

Directions

1. Shred the chicken into a bowl and mix with onion.
2. Add the rest of the ingredients to a bowl, mix and adjust seasoning.
3. Add chicken, mix and serve with crackers.

Nutrition Per Serving: Kcal 179 | Sodium 201 mg | Protein 15.9 g | Carbs 3.8 g | Fat 9 g | Potassium: 109 mg

14. Refried Pinto Bean Dip

Preparation time: 10 minutes | Cooking time: 10 minutes | Serving: 4

Ingredients

- 2 minced garlic cloves
- Red pepper flakes: ¼ tsp.
- Water: half cup
- 1 can of (30 oz.) Pinto beans, rinsed
- Cumin: 1 tsp.
- Chili powder: half tsp.
- Low-fat Mexican cheese blend: 1 cup
- Light sour cream: half cup
- Salt & pepper, to taste
- Cream cheese: half cup, low-fat

Directions

1. In a food processor, add water, garlic and beans. Pulse until mashed. Transfer to a pan on medium flame.
2. Add the seasoning and cook until heated through.
3. Add the rest of the ingredients with only half a cup of Mexican cheese. Cook for a few minutes.
4. Transfer to a bowl, add the rest of the cheese on top.
5. Microwave until cheese melts. Serve.

Nutrition Per Serving: Kcal 287 | Sodium 301 mg | Protein 9 g | Carbs 13 g | Fat 10 g | Potassium: 302 mg

15. Chocolate Peanut Butter Protein Balls

Preparation time: 10 minutes | Cooking time: 0 minutes | Serving: 12

Ingredients

- Cacao protein powder: 1.05 oz.
- Non-fat Greek yogurt: half cup
- Oat bran: 1 ½ cups
- Smooth peanut butter: 2 tbsp., no sugar or salt added

Directions

1. In a bowl, add all ingredients. Mix until combined.
2. Make into 12 balls. Keep in the fridge for half an hour.

Nutrition Per Serving: Kcal 89 | Sodium 13 mg | Protein 5.56 g | Carbs 8.3 g | Fat 3.27 g | Potassium: 302 mg

16. Roasted Chickpeas

Preparation time: 10 minutes | Cooking time: 40 minutes | Serving: 6

Ingredients

- Canola oil: 1 tbsp.
- 1 can of chickpeas, rinsed

Garlic parmesan

- Nutritional yeast & garlic powder: 2 tsp., each
- Canola oil: 1 tbsp.

Directions

1. Let the oven preheat to 400 F. Remove the chickpeas' skin as much as you can easily.
2. Pat dry the chickpeas and spread them on a baking sheet, toss with oil.
3. Bake for 35 to 40 minutes. Shaking the tray halfway through. They need to be hard upon pressing.
4. In a bowl, add the rest of the ingredients. Add the roasting chickpeas, toss well and serve.

Nutrition Per Serving: Kcal 99 | Sodium 31 mg | Protein 10 g | Carbs 9 g | Fat 1 g | Potassium: 42 mg

17. Chicken-Crusted Southwestern Pizza Rolls

Preparation time: 10 minutes | Cooking time: 25 minutes | Serving: 6

Ingredients

- Ground chicken: 1 lb.
- Taco seasoning: 1 pack, low-sodium

Toppings

- Onion: half cup, diced
- 1 can of (10 oz.) Tomatoes & green chilies, diced & drained
- Diced red bell pepper: half cup
- Olive oil: 1 tbsp.
- 2 to 3 cloves of minced garlic
- Skim cheddar cheese: half cup
- Black beans: half cup, rinsed
- Fresh cilantro: ¼ cup, chopped

Directions

1. Let the oven preheat to 425 F. Oil spray a 9 by 13".
2. In a bowl, add chicken and taco seasoning, mix. Spread thinly on the baking sheet and bake for 10 minutes.
3. Sauté onion and bell peppers in hot oil over high heat. Cook until lightly charred.
4. Add garlic and cook for 30 seconds, turn the heat off.
5. Onto the baked chicken, add the rest of the ingredients and press down.
6. Roll tightly with the help of parchment. Slice into one" rolls.
7. Bake for 5 to 10 minutes at 425 F.
8. Serve.

Nutrition Per Serving: Kcal 232 | Sodium 109 mg | Protein 21 g | Carbs 11 g | Fat 9 g | Potassium: 201 mg

18. Grilled Asparagus

Preparation time: 10 minutes | Cooking time: 8 minutes | Serving: 4

Ingredients

- Salt & pepper to taste.
- Olive oil: 1 tbsp.
- 1 bunch of asparagus, trimmed
- Garlic powder: 1 tsp.

Directions

1. Spread asparagus on a foil-lined baking tray, toss with the rest of the ingredients.
2. Place the foil onto the preheated grill, cook for 2 to 3 minutes with the lid closed.
3. Toss and cook for 3 to 4 minutes more. Serve.

Nutrition Per Serving: Kcal 66 | Sodium 87 mg | Protein 2 g | Carbs 11 g | Fat 9 g | Potassium: 201 mg

19. Buffalo Chicken Dip

Preparation time: 10 minutes | Cooking time: 3 hours & 25 minutes | Serving: 6

Ingredients

- White onion: 1 cup, chopped
- Yogurt cream cheese : 8 oz., softened
- Chicken broth: 2 cups
- Buffalo sauce: ¼ cup
- 1 lb., chicken breast, boneless & skinless
- Bleu cheese: half cup, crumbled
- Black pepper: 1 tsp.

Directions

1. In a slow cooker, add onion, black pepper, broth and chicken breast. Cook for 3 hours on high.
2. Let the oven preheat to 350 F.
3. Shred the chicken and add mix with the rest of the ingredients except for cheese.
4. Transfer to a baking dish, top with blue cheese. Bake for 25 minutes.
5. Serve.

Nutrition Per Serving: Kcal 265 | Sodium 121 mg | Protein 21 g | Carbs 6 g | Fat 13 g | Potassium: 228 mg

20. Veggie Stackers

Preparation time: 10 minutes | Cooking time: 0 minutes | Serving: 6

Ingredients

- 6 slices of skim mozzarella
- 6 fresh basil leaves
- 12 slices of cucumber
- Light Italian dressing: 1/3 cup
- 6 slices of a large tomato

- 6 slices of red onion

Directions

1. On each slice of tomato, add a cheese slice. Pour half the dressing on top.
2. Add onion slice, cucumber slices (2), then basil. Add the rest of the dressing.
3. Place a toothpick to secure in place. Serve.

Nutrition Per Serving: Kcal 135| Sodium 311 mg | Protein 7 g | Carbs 6 g | Fat 9 g | Potassium: 217 mg

---

21. Breakfast Cookies

Preparation time: 15 minutes | Cooking time: 40 minutes | Serving: 10

Ingredients

- 1 Egg
- 1 shredded Zucchini
- Melted Coconut Oil: ¼ cup
- 1 Banana
- Maple Syrup: 1 tbsp.
- Cinnamon: 1 tsp.
- Oats: ¾ cup
- Ground Flax Seed: 1 tbsp.
- Baking Powder: 1 tsp.
- Blueberries: half cup
- Hemp Seeds: 2 tbsp.
- Unflavored Protein Powder: 1/3 cup
- Almond Flour: ¾ cup

Directions

1. Let the oven preheat to 325 F.
2. Mash the banana and mix with zucchini, egg, maple syrup and coconut oil.
3. Add the rest of the ingredients (except for blueberries) to a bowl; mix.
4. Add the dry to wet ingredients, mix until combined. Add blueberries and fold.
5. With a scooper, place the batter on a parchment-lined baking tray.
6. Bake for 20 to 35 or 40 minutes. Serve.

Nutrition Per Serving: Kcal 127| Sodium 8.8 mg | Protein 4.9 g | Carbs 10.2 g | Fat 7.3 g | Potassium: 207 mg

---

22. Edamame Avocado Hummus

Preparation time: 15 minutes | Cooking time: 0 minutes | Serving: 8

Ingredients

- Half avocado
- Lemon juice: 1 tbsp.
- 2 minced garlic clove
- Avocado oil: 2 tbsp.
- Shelled edamame: 1 cup
- Tahini: 1 tsp.
- Onion powder: half tsp.
- Ground pepper: 1/8 tsp.
- Salt, a pinch

Directions

1. In a food processor, add all ingredients except for oil.
2. Pulse until smooth while the machine is running, gradually add oil.
3. Serve.

Nutrition Per Serving: Kcal 227| Sodium 111 mg | Protein 11 g | Carbs 2 g | Fat 3 g | Potassium: 271 mg

---

23. Oven-Roasted Carrots

Preparation time: 15 minutes | Cooking time: 55 minutes | Serving: 6

Ingredients

- Olive oil: 2 tbsp.
- Kosher salt: half tsp.
- Dried oregano: half tsp.
- Baby carrots: 1 lb.
- Honey: 1 tsp.
- Dried parsley: 1 tbsp.
- Black pepper: ¼ tsp.

Directions

1. Let the oven preheat to 375 F.
2. Add all ingredients to a bowl, toss well.
3. Spread on a parchment-lined baking tray. Loosely cover with foil, bake for 45 minutes.
4. Take the foil off and bake for 10 minutes.
5. Serve.

Nutrition Per Serving: Kcal 234| Sodium 120 mg | Protein 2 g | Carbs 3 g | Fat 2 g | Potassium: 201 mg

---

24. Spinach Artichoke Dip

Preparation time: 15 minutes | Cooking time: 45 minutes | Serving: 12

Ingredients

- 0% yogurt: half cup
- Low-fat fontina cheese: 1 cup, shredded
- 1 peeled clove of garlic
- Frozen spinach: 16 oz.
- Low-fat parmesan cheese: half cup, grated
- 1 can of (15 oz.) Artichoke in water, drained
- Avocado mayo: half cup
- Salt & pepper: 1/8 tsp., each

Directions

1. Let the oven preheat to 350 F.
2. Squeeze the spinach well.
3. Cut the artichokes in halves.
4. In a food processor, add parmesan cheese, mayo, salt, garlic, pepper, artichoke (1/3)

and yogurt. Pulse until combined, transfer to a bowl.
5. Add the rest of the ingredients (except for fontina cheese (1/4)) and mix.
6. Take an oven dish (1.5 qt.) and add the mixture. Spread evenly and top with fontina cheese.
7. Bake for 20 minutes, covered with foil. Take the foil off and bake for 20 to 25 minutes.
8. Broil for 5 minutes. Cool slightly and serve.

Nutrition Per Serving: Kcal 139 | Sodium 274 mg | Protein 6 g | Carbs 2 g | Fat 11 g | Potassium: 167 mg

25. Bacon Cheeseburger Meatballs

Preparation time: 15 minutes | Cooking time: 35 minutes | Serving: 8

Ingredients

- 1 egg
- Salt & pepper: ¼ tsp.
- 1 small zucchini, grated
- Lean ground turkey: 1 lb.
- 1 small yellow onion, diced
- Low-fat cheddar cheese: half cup, shredded
- Smoked paprika: 1 tsp.
- Bacon bits: 1/3 cup
- Garlic Powder: half tsp.

Everything Sauce

- Unsweetened relish: 2 tbsp.
- Yellow mustard: ¼ cup
- Low-sugar ketchup: half cup
- Light mayo: ¼ cup

Directions

1. Let the oven preheat to 350 F.
2. In a bowl, add all the ingredients, mix until combined.
3. Make the mixture into 16 balls and place it on a parchment-lined baking sheet.
4. Bake for half an hour.
5. In a bowl, add the rest of the sauce's ingredients, mix well and serve with the meatballs.

Nutrition Per Serving: Kcal 219 | Sodium 114 mg | Protein 12 g | Carbs 2 g | Fat 11 g | Potassium: 217 mg

26. Strawberry Lemon Popsicles

Preparation time: 4 hours & 15 minutes | Cooking time: 0 minutes | Serving: 2

Ingredients

- Powdered monk fruit sweetener, to taste
- Fresh strawberries: 1 cup
- Lemon juice: ¼ cup
- Water, as needed

Directions

1. Add all the ingredients to a blender. Pulse until smooth.
2. Pour into the molds, freeze for 4 hours. Serve.

Nutrition Per Serving: Kcal 67 | Sodium 4 mg | Protein 1 g | Carbs 0 g | Fat 2 g | Potassium: 101 mg

27. Cajun Cauliflower Rice

Preparation time: 15 minutes | Cooking time: 15 minutes | Serving: 4

Ingredients

- Cauliflower rice: 6 cups
- Andouille sausage (cajun style): 13 oz., sliced
- Salt & pepper to taste
- 1 diced bell pepper
- 1 diced yellow onion
- Olive oil: 2 tbsp.
- Cajun seasoning: 1 tbsp.

Directions

1. In a pan, saute onion and bell peppers in hot oil until tender-crisp.
2. Add sausage and cook for 3 to 4 minutes.
3. Add cauliflower rice and seasoning; keep stirring for 5 minutes.
4. Adjust seasoning and serve.

Nutrition Per Serving: Kcal 89 | Sodium 76 mg | Protein 1 g | Carbs 5 g | Fat 2 g | Potassium: 111 mg

28. Crustless Quiche

Preparation time: 15 minutes | **Cooking time:** 37 minutes | **Serving:** 6

Ingredients

- 5 oz. Mushrooms, sliced
- 1 diced small Onion
- Shredded Cheddar cheese: half cup
- Kale: half lb., chopped without ribs
- 1 cup of Water
- 2 tbsp. of Butter
- Dried thyme: half tsp.
- 1/4 cup of Ricotta cheese
- 3 cloves of Garlic, minced
- 6 Eggs
- Lemon zest: 1 tbsp.
- Low-fat Heavy cream: half cup
- 1 tsp. of Sea salt

Directions

1. Select sauté in an instant pot, add butter and sauté thyme, garlic, mushrooms and onion for 10 minutes.
2. Add kale and sauté for 2 minutes. Select cancel.
3. Oil spray a 1.5 qt. Glass baking dish that will fit inside the instant pot.
4. Whisk eggs with cream. Add kale mixture, salt, zest and cheddar (3/4). Mix until combined.
5. Transfer to the baking dish and top with ricotta cover with the lid.
6. Add one cup of water to the instant pot, place the dish on top of the trivet. Seal the valve.
7. Select 20 minutes. Release the pressure.
8. Cool slightly and serve.

Nutrition Per Serving: Kcal 260 | Sodium 76 mg | Protein 12 g | Carbs 7.1 g | Fat 20.9 g | Potassium: 111 mg

29. 3 Ingredient Protein Bites

Preparation time: 15 minutes | **Cooking time:** 0 minutes | **Serving:** 10-12

Ingredients

- Liquid sweetener: 1 tbsp., optional
- 1/3 cup of peanut butter
- 1 cup of almond flour
- 1 scoop of vanilla protein powder

Directions

1. Add all ingredients to a bowl, and mix.
2. Make the mixture into balls of 1 tbsp. Keep them in the fridge and serve.

Nutrition Per Serving: Kcal 187 | Sodium 56 mg | Protein 12 g | Carbs 2 g | Fat 9 g | Potassium: 110 mg

30. Pumpkin Cheesecake Pudding Parfaits

Preparation time: 15 minutes | **Cooking time:** 0 minutes | **Serving:** 8

Ingredients

- Instant cheesecake pudding mix: 1 pack, sugar-free
- Skim milk: 1 1/2 cups
- Pumpkin pie spice: half tsp.
- Vanilla Greek yogurt: 16 oz., low-fat
- Light cream cheese: 4 oz.,
- Pumpkin puree: 1 cup

Walnut layer
- Sugar: 2 tbsp.
- Walnuts: half cup

Directions

1. In a bowl, add all ingredients and mix with a hand mixer for 1 to 2 minutes.
2. Keep in the fridge for 10 to 15 minutes, covered with plastic wrap.
3. In a food processor, add sugar and walnuts, pulse until chopped.
4. In each serving glass, add pudding, then the walnut layer, top with pudding on top.
5. Serve.

Nutrition Per Serving: Kcal 256 | Sodium 123 mg | Protein 7 g | Carbs 3 g | Fat 10 g | Potassium: 120 mg

31. Healthy Cheeseburger Bites

Preparation time: 15 minutes | **Cooking time:** 25 minutes | **Serving:** 24

Ingredients

- 4 egg whites
- Breadcrumbs: half cup
- Fat-Free Shredded Cheddar: half cup
- Dill Pickles: 1.7 oz., diced
- Lean Ground Beef: 1 lb.
- Low-Sugar Ketchup: ¼ cup
- Shredded Parmesan: half cup
- Mustard: 3 tbsp.

Directions

1. Let the oven preheat to 400 F.
2. Oil spray 24 muffin cups.
3. In a pan, brown the beef on medium heat.
4. Add the rest of the ingredients to a bowl. Mix and add to the browned beef.
5. Cook for a few minutes and transfer to the muffin cups.
6. Bake for 23 to 25 minutes.

Nutrition Per Serving: Kcal 48| Sodium 113 mg | Protein 6.8 g | Carbs 2.3 g | Fat 1.3 g | Potassium: 121 mg

32. 5 Minute Cauliflower Ricotta Bake

Preparation time: 10 minutes| Cooking time: 5 minutes| Serving: 1

Ingredients

- Tomato sauce: ¼ cup, sugar-free
- Cauliflower rice: 1/3 cup
- Low-fat ricotta cheese: half cup

Directions

1. In a bowl, add all the ingredients and mix. Microwave for 3 to 4 minutes on high.
2. Serve.

Nutrition Per Serving: Kcal 78| Sodium 67 mg | Protein 4 g | Carbs 2 g | Fat 5 g | Potassium: 101 mg

33. Crab Rangoon Dip

Preparation time: 10 minutes| Cooking time: 0 minutes| Serving: 8

Ingredients

- Chopped scallions: 1 tbsp.
- Cream cheese: 8 oz., softened
- Crab meat: 2 cups
- Stevia: ¼ tsp.
- Light mayonnaise: 2 tsp.
- Black pepper: ¼ tsp.
- Half lemon's juice
- Shredded mozzarella cheese: 1 cup
- Diced pimentos: ¼ cup, drained
- Coconut aminos: 2 tsp.
- Garlic powder: half tsp.
- Salt, to taste

Directions

1. Let the oven preheat to 350 F.
2. In a bowl, add all ingredients except for a half cup of mozzarella. Mix and transfer to an oil sprayed 8 by 4" baking dish. Top with the rest of the cheese.
3. Bake for 20 minutes, serve.

Nutrition Per Serving: Kcal 357| Sodium 227 g | Protein 13 g | Carbs 8 g | Fat 22 g | Potassium: 278 mg

34. Smoked Salmon Dip

Preparation time: 10 minutes| Cooking time: 0 minutes| Serving: 6-10

Ingredients

- Low-fat cream cheese: 7 oz.
- Lemon juice: 1 to 2 tbsp.
- Mayonnaise: ¼ cup
- Lemon zest: 1 ½ tsp.
- Fresh dill: ¼ cup, chopped
- Smoked salmon: 7 oz.
- Half minced garlic clove
- Sour cream: ¼ cup
- Salt & pepper, to taste

Directions

1. In a food processor, add all ingredients except for salt & lemon juice. Mix until combined.
2. Taste, add lemon juice and salt to taste. Mix again and serve.

Nutrition Per Serving: Kcal 145| Sodium 507 g | Protein 5.1 g | Carbs 8 g | Fat 13 g | Potassium: 75 mg

35. Cheesy Stuffed Acorn Squash

Preparation time: 10 minutes| Cooking time: 20 minutes| Serving: 4

Ingredients

- Ground turkey breast: 1 pound
- 1 cup of sliced mushrooms
- Oregano: 1 tsp.
- 1 cup of diced celery
- 2 acorn squash, cut in half without seeds
- Basil: 1 tsp.
- 1 cup of diced onion
- Salt: 1/8 tsp.
- Black pepper, a pinch
- Cheddar cheese: 1 cup, low-fat
- Garlic powder: 1 tsp.
- Tomato sauce: 8 oz.

Directions

1. Let the oven preheat to 350 F.
2. In a glass dish, add the squash round side up. Microwave for 20 minutes, on high.

3. Brown the turkey in a pan. Add onion and celery, sauté until tender.
4. Add mushrooms and cook for 2 to 3 minutes. Add the rest of the ingredients and cook for few minutes.
5. Spoon the mixture into squash and cover with foil.
6. Bake for 15 minutes. Add some cheese on top, bake for few minutes till cheese melts.
7. Serve.

Nutrition Per Serving: Kcal 299 | Sodium 407 g | Protein 30 g | Carbs 38 g | Fat 4 g | Potassium: 176 mg

36. Egg Bites

Preparation time: 15 minutes | Cooking time: 7 minutes | Serving: 6

Ingredients

- 1/4 cup of cottage cheese
- 4 eggs
- Grated cheese: 1 tbsp.
- 1/4 bell pepper, diced
- Salt & pepper to taste
- Ham: 3 slices, chopped

Directions

1. Whisk eggs with cheese, then add bell pepper and ham.
2. Add salt and pepper.
3. Pour into the silicon muffin mold.
4. Add water (2 cups) to the instant pot with a trivet. Place the mold on the trivet.
5. Cook for 6 minutes, release the pressure and serve.

Nutrition Per Serving: Kcal 120 | Sodium 79.5 mg | Protein 7.9 g | Carbs 3 g | Fat 5.8 g | Potassium: 109 mg

37. Turkey Roll-Ups

Preparation time: 15 minutes | Cooking time: 0 minutes | Serving: 6

Ingredients

- 6 pretzels, gluten-free
- Turkey breast (oven roasted): 6 slices
- Goat cheese: 3 oz.
- Apple: 12 slices thinly cut

Directions

1. On each turkey slice, spread 1 tbsp. of goat cheese and put an apple slice in the center. Roll and place the pretzel in the middle
2. Serve.

Nutrition Per Serving: Kcal 134 | Sodium 121 g | Protein 14 g | Carbs 11 g | Fat 6 g | Potassium: 156 mg

38. Blueberry Mug Cake

Preparation time: 15 minutes | Cooking time: 2 minutes | Serving: 1

Ingredients

- Double cream: 2 tbsp.
- Lemon juice: 2 tbsp.
- Coconut flour: 2 tbsp.
- 1 egg
- 10 to 12 blueberries
- Salt, a pinch
- Granulated erythritol: 2 tbsp.
- Vanilla extract: ¼ tsp.
- Baking powder: ¼ tsp.

Directions

1. In a bowl, whisk the egg with vanilla extract, juice and cream.
2. In a different bowl, add the dry ingredients. Mix the dry to wet ingredients, add blueberries and fold.
3. Transfer to a mug, microwave for 1 minute at 800 watts.
4. Cook until the center is set and not liquid.
5. Serve.

Nutrition Per Serving: Kcal 225 | Sodium 165 g | Protein 6 g | Carbs 8 g | Fat 4 g | Potassium: 153 mg

39. French Carrot Medley

Preparation time: 15 minutes | Cooking time: 3-6 hours | Serving: 6

Ingredients

- Orange juice: ¾ cup
- Sliced mushrooms: 4 oz.
- Leeks: 1 stalk, sliced
- Sliced carrots: 2 cups
- 4 stalks of celery, diced
- Salt & pepper, to taste
- Chopped onions: 2 tbsp.
- Dried dill weed: half tsp.
- Tarragon: 1 tsp.

For slurry

- Water: ¼ cup
- Cornstarch: 2 tsp.

Directions

1. In a slow cooker, add all ingredients except for slurry. Stir and cook for 2 hours on high, or 3 to 4 hours on low.
2. Add the slurry ingredients to a bowl, whisk well and pour in the slow cooker.

3. Cook for 5 minutes. Serve.

Nutrition Per Serving: Kcal 45 | Sodium 56 g | Protein 4.9 g | Carbs 3 g | Fat 3 g | Potassium: 106 mg

40. Smoked Salmon Appetizer

Preparation time: 15 minutes | Cooking time: 0 minutes | Serving: 6

Ingredients

- Chopped fresh chives: ¼ cup
- Cream cheese: 1 cup, low-fat
- Half lemon's zest
- 1/3 cup of light mayonnaise
- Smoked salmon: 7 oz.
- Black pepper: ¼ tsp.

Directions

1. Slice the salmon into small pieces. Add to a bowl, with the rest of the ingredients, mix and let it rest for 15 minutes.
2. Serve on lettuce leaves.

Nutrition Per Serving: Kcal 257 | Sodium 160 g | Protein 11 g | Carbs 24 g | Fat 9 g | Potassium: 145 mg

41. Low-Carb Shrimp Dip

Preparation time: 25 minutes | Cooking time: 0 minutes | Serving: 16

Ingredients

- Cooked shrimp: 2 cups, cut into 3/8" pieces
- Cream cheese: 8 oz., softened
- Chopped red bell pepper: 1 cup
- Lemon juice: 2 tsp.
- Beau monde seasoning: 2 tsp.
- Sour cream: ¾ cup, low-fat
- Dried dill weed: 2 tsp.
- Chopped scallions: half cup

Directions

1. In a food processor, add all ingredients except for bell pepper, scallions and shrimp.
2. Pulse until smooth. Add the rest of the ingredients and mix.
3. Keep in the fridge for 1 hour.
4. Serve with vegetables.

Nutrition Per Serving: Kcal 119 | Sodium 444 g | Protein 6 g | Carbs 6 g | Fat 8 g | Potassium: 158 mg

42. Spicy Salmon Poppers

Preparation time: 10 minutes | Cooking time: 20 minutes | Serving: 6

Ingredients

- 5 eggs
- Ground pork rinds: ¾ cup
- Salt: ¼ tsp.
- Garlic powder: ¾ tsp.
- Half jalapeño, chopped
- 1 tbsp. Of avocado oil
- 1/4 cup of light mayonnaise
- Dried dill: half tsp.
- 1/8 tsp. Each of black pepper & red pepper flakes
- Canned salmon: 24 oz.
- Cayenne pepper: 1/8 plus ¼ tsp.

Directions

1. In a bowl, add all ingredients except for oil. Mix and make into 24 balls and press flat.
2. In a pan, add oil and add 4 to 6 poppers; cook for 4 to 5 minutes.
3. Cook the rest and serve with sauce.

Nutrition Per Serving: Kcal 341 | Sodium 444 g | Protein 14 g | Carbs 1.4 g | Fat 15 g | Potassium: 158 mg

43. 10-Minute Tuna Rolls

Preparation time: 10 minutes | Cooking time: 0 minutes | Serving: 2

Ingredients

- 2 slices of avocado, diced
- Wild-Caught Yellowfin Tuna (in olive oil): 1 pouch
- ground cayenne, a pinch
- 1 tsp. of hot sauce
- 1 cucumber
- 1/8 tsp. each of salt & pepper

Directions

1. Cut the cucumber thinly lengthwise with a mandolin. Do not cut the seed.
2. Pat dry the cucumber slices.

3. Add the rest of the ingredients to a bowl, except for avocado and mix.
4. Spoon the mixture on cucumber slices and place the avocado on top.
5. Roll the slice and secure it with a toothpick.

Nutrition Per Serving: Kcal 122| Sodium 476 g | Protein 9.5 g | Carbs 2 g | Fat 8.8 g | Potassium: 158 mg

44. Tuna Stuffed Avocado

Preparation time: 15 minutes | Cooking time: 0 minutes | Serving: 2

Ingredients

- 1 avocado, halved
- Olive oil: 2 tsp.
- Sea salt & black pepper, to taste
- Diced red onion: 2 tbsp.
- Canned tuna in olive oil: 5 oz.
- Lime juice: 1 tbsp.
- Chopped cilantro: ¼ cup
- Mayo: 1 tbsp.

Directions

1. Shred the tuna after draining it.
2. Empty the avocado halves by scraping the flesh and leaving a shell.
3. Mash the avocado flesh and add the rest of the ingredients, and mix.
4. Use a large fork to thoroughly mash the avocado. Stuff the shells and serve with a drizzle of lime juice.

Nutrition Per Serving: Kcal 407| Sodium 320 g | Protein 19 g | Carbs 11 g | Fat 33 g | Potassium: 289 mg

Part 2: Meat & Poultry Recipes

1. Creamy Chicken Casserole

Preparation time: 15 minutes | Cooking time: 30 minutes | Serving: 8

Ingredients

- Panko breadcrumbs: half cup
- Cream of chicken soup: 1 can, low-fat
- Diced butternut squash: 1 cup
- Skim milk: half cup
- Ground chicken: 1 pound
- 1 peeled apple, diced
- Low-fat cheddar cheese: half cup, shredded

Directions

1. Let the oven preheat to 350 F.
2. Cook ground chicken in a pan until cooked through. Add milk and soup, cook, until it starts to bubble.
3. Add squash and apple, cook for 10 to 15 minutes.
4. Transfer to a baking dish, add bread crumbs and cheddar cheese on top.
5. Bake for ten minutes. Serve.

Nutrition Per Serving: Kcal 150 | Sodium 113 g | Protein 12 g | Carbs 8 g | Fat 7 g | Potassium: 418 mg

2. Chicken & Fennel en Papillote

Preparation time: 15 minutes | Cooking time: 20 minutes | Serving: 4

Ingredients

- 1 bulb fennel, sliced thin
- 8 chicken fillets
- Dill: 1 tbsp., chopped
- Lemon pepper: 1 tsp., no-salt-added
- Olive oil: half tbsp.
- 1 lemon, sliced

Directions

1. Let the oven preheat to 350 F
2. Take 4 sheets of parchment paper of 12 by 12".
3. In each parchment paper, add chicken and pat dry. Rub with olive oil, and sprinkle with lemon pepper.
4. Add lemon slices, fennel and dill on top, fold the parchment and make it into a packet.
5. Bake for 18 to 20 minutes. Serve.

Nutrition Per Serving: Kcal 155.7 | Sodium 124.3 g | Protein 18 g | Carbs 5.1 g | Fat 6.3 g | Potassium: 308 mg

3. Teriyaki Beef Skewers

Preparation time: 15 minutes | Cooking time: 20 minutes | Serving: 2

Ingredients

- Rice vinegar: 1 tbsp.
- Diced Onion: half cup
- 1 minced Garlic Clove
- Tamari: 2 tbsp.
- Lean steak: 8 oz., cubed
- 8 Cherry tomatoes
- Diced Red bell pepper: half cup
- Pineapple chunks: ¼ cup
- 6 mushrooms, cut in half
- Olive oil: half tbsp.

Directions

1. Add ginger, tamari, cilantro, rice vinegar and garlic to a bowl. Mix and add steaks, mix and let it rest for 15 minutes.
2. Let the oven preheat to 375 F.
3. Add the vegetables to a bowl and toss with oil.
4. Thread the steaks and vegetables onto soaked skewers alternatively.
5. Bake for 20 minutes; after ten minutes, flip the skewers.

Nutrition Per Serving: Kcal 140 | Sodium 295 g | Protein 16.4 g | Carbs 12 g | Fat 3.7 g | Potassium: 316 mg

4. Chipotle Chicken Fajita Bowls

Preparation time: 10 minutes | Cooking time: 20 minutes | Serving: 4

Ingredients

For Chicken

- Chipotle powder: half to 1 tsp.
- Chicken breast: 1 to 1.5 lbs
- Garlic salt: 1 tsp.
- Half lime's juice
- Tomato paste: 2 tbsp.
- Salt & pepper, to taste
- Olive oil: 2 tbsp.

For vegetables

- Garlic salt: 1 tsp.
- 1 sweet onion, sliced
- 1 red, 1 yellow, 1 orange & 1 green bell pepper, sliced
- Cumin: 1 tsp.
- Olive oil: 1 tbsp.
- Riced cauliflower: 4 cups, cooked (for serving)

Directions

1. In a bowl, add all ingredients of chicken, except for chicken. Mix and add the chicken; coat well.
2. In a pan, add oil and place on medium-high heat.
3. Saute onion for 1 to 2 minutes, add the rest of the vegetables' ingredients. Cook for 4 to 5 minutes.
4. In a pan, add oil and cook chicken for 4 to 5 minutes on 1 side.
5. In serving bowls, add cauliflower rice, fajita vegetables and chicken. Serve.

Nutrition Per Serving: Kcal 356 | Sodium 258 g | Protein 41 g | Carbs 12 g | Fat 7 g | Potassium: 371 mg

5. Chili with Ground Beef

Preparation time: 10 minutes | Cooking time: 50 minutes | Serving: 4

Ingredients

- Water: 8 cups or more
- 2 onions, diced
- Ground chuck: 2 pounds
- Dry kidney beans: 16 oz., rinsed
- Olive oil: 2 tbsp.
- 3 cloves garlic, minced
- Oregano: 1 tbsp.
- Canned diced tomatoes: 28 oz., in juice
- 1 green bell pepper, chopped
- Tomato paste: 6 oz.
- Salt and pepper, to taste
- Chili powder: 3-4 tbsp.
- Beef broth: 32 oz.
- Ground cumin: 2-3 tbsp.

Directions

1. In an electric cooker, add beans and water. Cook for 20 minutes on high pressure.
2. Drain and dry the cooker.
3. In a pan, add bell pepper, chuck, onion and garlic. Cook until browned.
4. Drain and add to the cooker with beans. Add water stir well.
5. Cook for half an hour on high pressure. Release the pressure.
6. Serve.

Nutrition Per Serving: Kcal 278 | Sodium 298 g | Protein 30 g | Carbs 17 g | Fat 7 g | Potassium: 404 mg

6. Southwestern Chicken Meatballs

Preparation time: 10 minutes | Cooking time: 15 minutes | Serving: 12

Ingredients

- 1 jalapeño, without seeds
- Half bell pepper, cut into chunks
- Panko crumbs: ¼ cup
- 2 cloves garlic
- A pinch of oregano
- 1 1/2 lbs. Of lean ground chicken
- 3 scallions, trimmed
- 1 egg
- Black pepper: ¼ tsp.
- Cumin: 1 tsp.
- Fresh cilantro: ¼ cup, chopped
- Sea salt: half tsp.

Directions

1. Let the oven preheat to 400 F.
2. In a food processor, add scallions, jalapeño, cilantro, red bell pepper and garlic. Pulse until minced.
3. In a bowl, add all ingredients, mix and make into balls. Place on a parchment-lined baking sheet.
4. Bake for 15 minutes. Serve.

Nutrition Per Serving: Kcal 67 | Sodium 178 g | Protein 10 g | Carbs 2.3 g | Fat 1.8 g | Potassium: 201 mg

7. Caprese Hasselback Chicken

Preparation time: 10 minutes | Cooking time: 25 minutes | Serving: 4

Ingredients

- Thinly sliced mozzarella cheese: 4 oz.
- Olive oil: 2 tbsp.
- 2 Roma tomatoes, sliced
- 4 chicken breasts: 6 oz., each
- Sea salt & pepper
- Fresh basil: ¼ cup, sliced
- Balsamic vinegar: 2 tbsp.

Directions

1. Let the oven preheat to 400 F.
2. In each chicken breast, make 5 to 6 slits, do not cut too deep.
3. Season the chicken with salt and pepper.
4. Add cheese, basil and tomatoes into the slits.
5. Drizzle balsamic vinegar and olive oil on top.
6. Bake for 20 to 25 minutes. Serve.

Nutrition Per Serving: Kcal 365| Sodium 218 g | Protein 39 g | Carbs 4 g | Fat 21 g | Potassium: 318 mg

8. Chicken Breast with Steamed Vegetables

Preparation time: 10 minutes | Cooking time: 20 minutes | Serving: 4

Ingredients

- Mixed Vegetables: 4 cups
- Chicken Breast: 12 oz., boneless & skinless
- Olive Oil: 8 tbsp.
- Salt & Pepper, to taste

Directions

1. Let the oven preheat to 400 F.
2. Coat the chicken in oil and season with salt and pepper.
3. Bake chicken for 15 to 20 minutes.
4. Slice the vegetables into bite-size pieces.
5. Steam in a steamer on medium flame.
6. Serve with chicken.

Nutrition Per Serving: Kcal 211| Sodium 111 g | Protein 13 g | Carbs 4 g | Fat 8 g | Potassium: 309 mg

9. Smoky Cabbage Rolls

Preparation time: 10 minutes | Cooking time: 30 minutes | Serving: 12

Ingredients

- 1 lb. Of ground turkey, lean
- 2 tbsp. Of smoked paprika
- Cauliflower rice: 1 cup
- 1 sweet onion, diced
- Garlic powder: half tsp.
- Salt & pepper: 1/4 tsp., each
- 12 cabbage leaves
- Canned whole tomatoes: 10 oz., unsalted
- Italian seasoning: half tsp.
- No-calorie sweetener: 1 tsp.
- Worcestershire sauce: 2 tbsp.
- Onion powder: half tsp.

Directions

1. let the oven preheat to 350 F.
2. Steam the cabbage leaves for 5 minutes until tender, transfer them to a bowl.
3. Oil spray a skillet and saute onion for 1 to 2 minutes on medium heat.
4. Add turkey and cook until browned.
5. Add all spices (except for garlic & onion powder) with 1 tbsp. of Worcestershire sauce, cook for 1 minute. Add cauliflower rice, cook for 2 minutes.
6. In a food processor, add garlic & onion powder, Worcestershire sauce and tomatoes with liquid. Pulse until chopped.
7. In each cabbage leaf, add meat mixture (2 oz.) place in a casserole dish.
8. Pour tomato mixture on top. Bake for 20 minutes.
9. Serve.

Nutrition Per Serving: Kcal 207| Sodium 117 g | Protein 14 g | Carbs 8 g | Fat 9 g | Potassium: 343 mg

10. Pork Street Tacos

Preparation time: 10 minutes | Cooking time: 2 hours & 30 minutes | Serving: 10-12

Ingredients

- Chipotle seasoning: 2 tbsp.
- 4 minced cloves garlic
- Canola oil: 2 tbsp.
- Boneless pork tenderloin: 2 pounds
- Chopped white onion: 1 cup
- Corn mini tortillas: 30 to 40

- 1½ cups of chicken broth
- Lime juice: ¼ cup
- 100% cranberry juice: 2 cups

Directions

1. Let the oven preheat to 350 F. Season the pork with chipotle seasoning.
2. Cook meat in a Dutch oven with oil for 7-8 minutes on each side. Take it out and set it aside.
3. Add onion and sauté for 4-5 minutes. Add garlic, cook for 1 minute.
4. Add the rest of the ingredients, deglaze the pan. Add meat back to the pan and let it simmer.
5. Simmer for 1 ½ hour in the oven, covered.
6. Take the lid off and cook for half an hour more. Take it out of the oven, shred it with forks.
7. Serve in warmed tortillas with sour cream and other desired toppings.

Nutrition Per Serving: Kcal 288| Sodium 201 g | Protein 31 g | Carbs 15 g | Fat 9.8 g | Potassium: 367 mg

11. Chicken Spinach & Tomato

Preparation time: 10 minutes| Cooking time: 20 minutes| Serving: 6

Ingredients

- Skinless & boneless chicken breast: 2½ pounds, 1-inch pieces
- Canned diced tomatoes: 15 oz.
- 2 minced garlic cloves
- Olive oil: 2 tbsp.
- Mushrooms: 8 oz., sliced
- Salt & pepper, to taste
- Baby spinach: 7 oz.

Directions

1. In a pan, add oil on medium flame.
2. Add garlic and chicken, sprinkle salt and pepper.
3. Cook until juices become clear.
4. Add mushrooms, tomatoes and spinach. Cook until it is reduced by half.
5. Adjust seasoning and serve.

Nutrition Per Serving: Kcal 173| Sodium 201 g | Protein 40 g | Carbs 8 g | Fat 6 g | Potassium: 367 mg

12. Low Carb Breakfast Burritos

Preparation time: 10 minutes| Cooking time: 20 minutes| Serving: 7

Ingredients

- Heavy cream: half cup
- 7 tortillas, low carb
- Low-fat white cheddar cheese: 1/4 cup, shredded
- 2 tbsp. Of butter
- 8 eggs
- Salt & pepper: half tsp., each
- 1 lb. Of bacon
- Low-fat cheddar cheese: 1 1/2 cups, shredded

Directions

1. Let the oven preheat to 350 F, oil spray a 9 by 13" baking dish.
2. Cook bacon until crispy and crumble into pieces.
3. In a bowl, whisk eggs with salt, cream and pepper.
4. In melted butter, add eggs on medium flame, cook until scrambled. Turn the heat off.
5. In each tortilla, add eggs, bacon and cheese mixture (leave ¼ cup of each cheese). Roll and place in the baking dish.
6. Sprinkle cheese mixture on top. Bake for 15 minutes, covered.

Nutrition Per Serving: Kcal 405| Sodium 219 g | Protein 40 g | Carbs 17 g | Fat 34 g | Potassium: 356 mg

13. Sour Cream Chicken Enchiladas

Preparation time: 10 minutes| Cooking time: 25 minutes| Serving: 7

Ingredients

- 3 tbsp. of butter
- Arrowroot powder: 3 tsp.
- 6 tsp. Of water
- 1 cup of sour cream
- Kosher salt: half tsp.
- 2 cups of chicken broth
- Oregano: ¼ tsp.
- Chopped green chiles: 4 oz.
- Colby-jack cheese: 2 cups, grated
- Chipotle chili powder: 1/8 tsp.
- 3 chicken breast, boneless & skinless: halved
- Riced cauliflower: 3 cups

Directions

1. In a pan, melt butter.

2. Mix the cold water with arrowroot and add to the pan.
3. Add chicken broth, cook for 2-3 minutes until thickens.
4. Add the spices and cook for 30 seconds.
5. Add chicken to the pan, let it simmer for 15 minutes on low flame.
6. Take the chicken out and shred.
7. Add sour cream to the pan, add chicken to the pan with cauliflower rice.
8. Mix well and simmer for 5 minutes, covered.
9. Add cheese on top and cook until cheese melts. Serve.

Nutrition Per Serving: Kcal 267 | Sodium 209 g | Protein 21 g | Carbs 11 g | Fat 12 g | Potassium: 360 mg

14. Healthy Orange Chicken

Preparation time: 10 minutes | Cooking time: 45 minutes | Serving: 4

Ingredients

- Fresh ginger: 1 tbsp.
- Toasted sesame oil: 2 tbsp.
- Coconut aminos: ¼ cup
- 4 chicken breasts, boneless & skinless, cubed
- Chicken broth: half cup
- Orange juice: 2 ½ cups
- Honey: 3 tbsp.
- Garlic powder: 1 tsp.
- Orange zest: 1 tbsp.
- Pepper: 1 tsp.
- Steamed green beans: 4 cups (for serving)

Directions

1. In a pan, add oil on medium flame. Cook chicken for 12-15 minutes.
2. Take it out on a plate.
3. Add the rest of the ingredients to a bowl, and mix. Add to the same pan and cook for 15 to 20 minutes.
4. As the sauce thickens, add chicken and toss well.
5. Serve with steamed beans.

Nutrition Per Serving: Kcal 362 | Sodium 229 g | Protein 28 g | Carbs 39 g | Fat 10 g | Potassium: 344 mg

15. Asian Chicken Lettuce Wraps

Preparation time: 10 minutes | Cooking time: 45 minutes | Serving: 4

Ingredients

- Cooking wine: 3 tbsp.
- Soy sauce: 2 tsp., low-sodium
- Hoisin sauce: 2 tbsp.
- Sugar substitute: ¼ tsp.
- 1 can of (8 oz.) Water chestnuts, minced
- Peanut butter: 1 tbsp.
- Sriracha: 2 tsp.
- Minced garlic: 1 tbsp.
- 8 butter lettuce, small leaves
- Ground chicken breast: half pound
- Minced onion: 1 cup
- Toasted sesame oil: 1 tsp.
- 1 cucumber, sliced into 1-inch strips with seeds
- Minced ginger: 1 tsp.
- Salt: ¼ tsp.
- 1 scallion, chopped

Directions

1. In a bowl, add soy sauce, sugar substitute, water chestnuts, bamboo shoots, peanut butter, sherry, sriracha and hoisin sauce. Mix well.
2. Oil spray a pan on medium heat. Saute onion for 4 minutes.
3. Add garlic and cook for 1 minute.
4. Add chicken, salt and ginger cook until no longer pink. Add peanut butter mixture. Cook for 2 minutes.
5. Add sesame oil. Serve in lettuce leaves, with cucumber and scallions on top.
6. Serve.

Nutrition Per Serving: Kcal 155 | Sodium 637 g | Protein 16 g | Carbs 33 g | Fat 4 g | Potassium: 456 mg

16. Chicken Crust Pizza

Preparation time: 10 minutes | Cooking time: 25 minutes | Serving: 8

Ingredients

- Sliced Mushrooms: 1 cup
- Ground Chicken: 16 oz.
- Parmesan Cheese: 1 cup, shredded
- Stewed Tomatoes with Basil, Oregano & garlic: half cup
- Onion powder & garlic powder: 1 tbsp., each
- Sliced Black Olives, as needed
- Splenda: 1 tsp.
- Skim Mozzarella: 1 cup, shredded
- 5 Sweet Mini Peppers
- Oregano: 1 tbsp.
- 3 Garlic

Directions

1. Let the oven preheat to 450 F.
2. In a bowl, add chicken, half a cup of each cheese. Mix and add Italian seasoning, Oregano, salt, Garlic powder, pepper and onion powder mix and spread on an oil sprayed parchment-lined baking sheet.
3. Bake for 12 to 15 minutes.
4. In a food processor, add the rest of the ingredients except for cheese & toppings.
5. Spread over the baked crust, add topping and cheese.
6. Bake for 6 to 10 minutes, slice & serve.

Nutrition Per Serving: Kcal 190 | Sodium 502 g | Protein 20 g | Carbs 5.3 g | Fat 9.7 g | Potassium: 456 mg

17. Parmesan Chicken Nuggets

Preparation time: 10 minutes | Cooking time: 15 minutes | Serving: 4

Ingredients

- Skim parmesan cheese: half cup
- Salt: half tsp.
- 1/4 cup of cold water
- 1 lb. Chicken breasts: boneless & skinless, cut into pieces
- Panko breadcrumbs: 1 cup
- Pepper: 1/8 tsp.

Directions

1. Let the oven preheat to 400 F.
2. Add all ingredients (only half the cheese) to a food processor, except for bread crumbs. Pulse until combined. Make into nuggets.
3. In a bowl, add cheese and bread crumbs. Coat the nuggets in this mixture and place them on the parchment-lined baking sheet.
4. Oil spray the nuggets and bake for 12 to 15 minutes.
5. Serve.

Nutrition Per Serving: Kcal 205 | Sodium 289 g | Protein 30 g | Carbs 10 g | Fat 8 g | Potassium: 376 mg

18. Asian Pork Tenderloin

Preparation time: 10 minutes | Cooking time: 3-4 hours/ 40 minutes | Serving: 4

Ingredients

- 1/3 cup of brown sugar substitute
- Pepper: 1 ½ tsp.
- 2 tbsp. of lemon juice
- 1/3 cup of light soy sauce
- 2 tbsp. of rice vinegar
- 2 pounds of pork tenderloin
- 1 tbsp. of dry mustard
- 2 tbsp. of Worcestershire sauce
- 1 tbsp. of ginger
- 4 minced garlic cloves

Directions

1. In a ziplock bag, add all the ingredients, except for tenderloin.
2. Mix and add tenderloin. Keep in the fridge overnight.
3. Bake at 375 F for 30 to 40 minutes or cook in a slow cooker for 4-6 hours.

Nutrition Per Serving: Kcal 256 | Sodium 658 g | Protein 34 g | Carbs 9 g | Fat 9 g | Potassium: 269 mg

19. Stuffed Peppers

Preparation time: 10 minutes | Cooking time: 4-8 hours | Serving: 6

Ingredients

- 1 lb. Of ground turkey
- Garlic powder: half tsp.
- Diced sweet onion: half cup
- 6 bell peppers
- Cooked rice: 1 ½ cups
- Salt: 1 tsp.
- Pepper: ¼ tsp.
- Canned tomato sauce: 12 oz.
- Worcestershire sauce: 1 ½ tsp.
- Dried herbs: 1 tsp.
- ¼ cup of water

Directions

1. Slice the top off of bell peppers and take the seeds, membrane out.
2. In a bowl, add turkey, salt, cooked rice, onion, dried herbs (half tsp.), garlic powder

(1/4 tsp.), and Worcestershire sauce (1 tsp.). Mix well.
3. Spoon into the bell peppers and cover with tops.
4. In a slow cooker, add water (1/4 cup) to the bottom. Place bell peppers and cook for 8 hours on low or 4 hours on high.
5. When 30 minutes are remaining, add the rest of the ingredients to a bowl.
6. Take the bell pepper top and spoon the mixture on top. Cook for 30 minutes.
7. Before serving, make a cut in the bottom to drip any liquid from bell pepper.
8. Serve.

Nutrition Per Serving: Kcal 342 | Sodium 733 g | Protein 25 g | Carbs 49 g | Fat 4 g | Potassium: 758 mg

20. Chicken Japchae

Preparation time: 20 minutes | Cooking time: 20 minutes | Serving: 4

Ingredients

- Dry Angel Hair Noodles: 7 oz., cooked
- Toasted Sesame Seeds: 1 tbsp.
- Baby Bok Choy: 2 heads, sliced
- Fresh Spinach: 1 cup, sliced
- 1 Chicken Breast, sliced thin
- 1 scallion: sliced
- 8 Dry Shitake Mushrooms
- Half sliced Onion
- Sesame oil
- Carrot: half cup, cut into Matchsticks

Marinade

- 1 mined clove of Garlic
- Rice Vinegar: ¼ cup
- Splenda: 2 tsp.
- White Pepper: half tsp.
- Light Soy Sauce: 2 tbsp. + ¼ cup
- Sesame oil: half tsp.

Directions

1. In a bowl, add all ingredients of marinade. Mix and save ¼ cup of it for later.
2. In the rest of the marinade, add chicken, mix and let it rest for 5 minutes.
3. Oil spray a wok and place on high heat. Add chicken without marinade and cook for 3-5 minutes. Take it out.
4. Oil spray the wok again and saute onion and carrots. Add marinade (1 tbsp.) And cook for 3-4 minutes, take it out on a plate.
5. Oil spray the wok again, cook mushrooms for 3 minutes. Add bok choy, spinach and marinade (1 tbsp.) Cook for 2 minutes, take it out on a plate.
6. Oil spray the wok again and cook eggs, and add cooked noodles, cook for 2 minutes. Add the rest of the reserved marinade and cook for 2 minutes.
7. Add scallion, sesame oil the rest of the ingredients, toss and serve.

Nutrition Per Serving: Kcal 144.5 | Sodium 689 g | Protein 14 g | Carbs 13.7 g | Fat 4.4 g | Potassium: 408 mg

21. Balsamic Roast Chicken

Preparation time: 10 minutes | Cooking time: 1 hour & 20 minutes | Serving: 8

Ingredients

- Balsamic vinegar: half cup
- Dried rosemary: 1 tsp.
- 1 garlic clove
- Fresh rosemary: 8 sprigs
- Brown sugar substitute: 1 tsp.
- Olive oil: 1 tbsp.
- Whole chicken: 4 pounds
- Black pepper: 1/8 tsp.

Directions

1. Let the oven preheat to 350 F.
2. Mince the garlic with rosemary. Rub the chicken with herb mixture and oil, sprinkle with black pepper.
3. Add 2 sprigs in the cavity and loosen the skin.
4. Bind the chicken with kitchen twine.
5. Roast the chicken for 20 to 25 minutes for each pound, such as for this chicken 1 hour & 20 minutes or until the internal temperature of the meat reaches 165 F.
6. Keep basting with pan juice.
7. Add the sugar and balsamic vinegar to a pan; heat to dissolve the sugar but do not boil.
8. Slice the chicken and serve with balsamic mixture.

Nutrition Per Serving: Kcal 364| Sodium 257 g | Protein 51 g | Carbs 4 g | Fat 16 g | Potassium: 408 mg

22. Chicken Sweet Potato Curry

Preparation time: 10 minutes| Cooking time: 2 hours| Serving: 4-6

Ingredients

- Curry powder: 4 tbsp.
- 2 peeled sweet potatoes, cubed
- 1 onion, sliced
- Chicken: 2 lbs., cut into pieces
- Salt & pepper to taste
- 1 cup of water

Directions

1. In a pot, add onion, water, chicken and curry powder. Stir well.
2. Simmer for 2 hours on low heat, covered. After 1 hour & 15 minutes, add potatoes and cover the pan.
3. Serve.

Nutrition Per Serving: Kcal 301| Sodium 222 g | Protein 33 g | Carbs 13 g | Fat 13 g | Potassium: 456 mg

23. Apple Baked Stuffed Pork Chops

Preparation time: 10 minutes| Cooking time: 50 minutes| Serving: 4

Ingredients

- Half sweet onion, diced
- Dried sage: 1 tsp.
- 1/4 cup cranberries, dried
- Olive oil: 1 tbsp.
- 4 pork chops, bone-in & thick-cut
- Half apple, chopped
- Salt & pepper, to taste

Directions

1. Let the oven preheat to 375 F.
2. Sauté onion in hot oil for 5 minutes. Add cranberries, sage and apples.
3. Cook for 8 to 10 minutes. Season with salt and pepper, turn the heat off.
4. Make slits on the pork chops and make a pocket, fill with the mixture and bake for half an hour. Serve.

Nutrition Per Serving: Kcal 250| Sodium 85.4 g | Protein 26.3 g | Carbs 5.7 g | Fat 13 g | Potassium: 506 mg

24. White Chicken Chili Verde

Preparation time: 10 minutes| Cooking time: 20 minutes| Serving: 4-6

Ingredients

- Minced garlic: 1 tbsp.
- 2 chicken breasts, boneless & skinless
- 1 bunch of cilantro
- 2 serrano peppers, without seeds
- Canned chicken broth: 32 oz.
- 2 anaheim peppers, without seeds
- 1 sweet onion, cut into rounds
- Water: 1-1 1/2 cups
- 2 chicken thighs, boneless & skinless
- Salt & pepper: half tsp., each
- 6 tomatillos, cut into fours
- Cumin: 1 tbsp.

Directions

1. In an instant pot, add all ingredients, stir and cook for 20 minutes on high pressure.
2. Release the pressure, take the chicken out and blend the rest of the chili with a stick blender.
3. Shred the chicken and add to the pot.
4. Add enough water to reach your desired consistency. Heat it through. Serve.

Nutrition Per Serving: Kcal 221| Sodium 768 g | Protein 27 g | Carbs 9 g | Fat 9 g | Potassium: 568 mg

25. Spanish Chicken and Bean Stew

Preparation time: 10 minutes| Cooking time: 30 minutes| Serving: 4

Ingredients

- 1 large Onion
- 1 tbsp. of Paprika
- Olive oil: 1 tbsp.
- Canned roasted diced tomato: 1 ½ cups
- 20 oz., chicken breast, boneless & skinless
- 2 cloves of garlic
- Chicken broth: 1 cup
- Salt & black pepper, to taste
- Fire-roasted Red Peppers: ¾ cup
- Artichoke Hearts in oil: 7 oz.
- 7 Stuffed Green Olives
- Pinto Beans: 1 1/2 cups
- 5 tbsp. of Parsley

Directions

1. In a pan, saute garlic and chopped onion in oil for 2 to 4 minutes.
2. Season the chicken with salt, pepper and paprika (half) add to the pan.
3. Cook for 4 to 6 minutes.

4. Add the rest of the ingredients, cook for 20 to 25 minutes, covered.
5. Serve.

Nutrition Per Serving: Kcal 409 | Sodium 705 g | Protein 38 g | Carbs 33.9 g | Fat 13.7 g | Potassium: 501 mg

26. Barbeque Chicken Pizza

Preparation time: 10 minutes | Cooking time: 20 minutes | Serving: 4

Ingredients

- 1 pizza crust, 12" thick
- Cooked chicken breast: 4 oz., sliced
- 8 bell pepper rings
- Mushrooms: 1 cup, sliced
- Tomato sauce: 1 cup, no salt added
- 1 tomato, cut into slices
- Low-fat mozzarella cheese: 1 cup, shredded
- Barbecue sauce: 4 tbsp.

Directions

1. Let the oven preheat to 400 F.
2. On the pizza crust, spread the sauce. Add the vegetables and chicken.
3. Add sauce and top with cheese.
4. Place in the oven, bake for 12 to 14 minutes.
5. Slice & serve.

Nutrition Per Serving: Kcal 384 | Sodium 740 g | Protein 21 g | Carbs 48 g | Fat 12 g | Potassium: 565 mg

27. Sesame Chicken

Preparation time: 10 minutes | Cooking time: 10 minutes | Serving: 4

Ingredients

- Cornstarch: 2 tbsp.
- Boneless & skinless chicken breasts: 1 pound, cubed
- Scallions, chopped
- Salt & pepper, a pinch of each
- Olive oil: 1 tbsp.

For sauce

- Honey: 2 tbsp.
- Sesame seeds: 2 tbsp.
- Soy sauce: 3 tbsp.
- Sriracha: 1 tsp., or more
- 1 clove of minced garlic
- Sesame oil: 1 tbsp.
- Grated ginger: 1 tsp.

Directions

1. Add all the sauce's ingredients to a bowl and mix.
2. Season the chicken with salt and pepper.
3. Cook chicken in hot oil for 5 to 6 minutes, add sauce and simmer for 3 to 4 minutes.
4. Serve with scallions on top.

Nutrition Per Serving: Kcal 270 | Sodium 913 g | Protein 21 g | Carbs 14 g | Fat 11 g | Potassium: 499 mg

28. Lemon Rosemary Chicken

Preparation time: 15 minutes | Cooking time: 30 minutes | Serving: 4

Ingredients

- 2 lemons, 1 sliced & 1 juiced
- Black pepper: ¼ tsp.
- Dried rosemary: 1 tbsp.
- Minced garlic: 1 tsp.
- Salt: half tsp.
- Chicken drumsticks: 1.5 lbs.
- 3 carrots, sliced into rounds
- 1/4 cup of olive oil
- 1 diced sweet potato

Directions

1. Let the oven preheat to 425 F
2. Add salt, pepper, oil, garlic, lemon juice and rosemary to a bowl and mix.
3. In a bowl, add sweet potatoes, chicken and carrots, toss with rosemary mixture.
4. Spread on a baking pan, add lemon slices on top.
5. Bake for half an hour until the chicken's internal temperature reaches 165 F.

Nutrition Per Serving: Kcal 309 | Sodium 603 g | Protein 25 g | Carbs 17 g | Fat 12.8 g | Potassium: 406 mg

29. Sheet Pan Pork Tenderloin Dinner

Preparation time: 15 minutes | Cooking time: 35 minutes | Serving: 4

Ingredients

- Pork tenderloin: 1 lb.
- Salt & pepper, to taste
- Brussels sprouts: 1 lb., halved
- 4 Yukon gold potatoes, cut into fours
- Chopped rosemary for serving
- Olive oil: 2 tbsp.

Directions

1. In a pan, add oil and sear the pork on all sides until browned.
2. Let the oven preheat to 425 F.
3. Toss the potatoes & Brussels in salt, oil and pepper, spread on a baking sheet.
4. Place pork in the center of the vegetables.
5. Bake for 15 to 20 minutes until the internal temperature of the meat reaches 145 F.
6. Take the Brussels and meat out, bake the potatoes at 450 F for 15 minutes.
7. Serve the pork with brussels sprouts and potatoes, topped with rosemary.

Nutrition Per Serving: Kcal 289 | Sodium 349 g | Protein 26 g | Carbs 7 g | Fat 12 g | Potassium: 411 mg

30. Chicken Pie

Preparation time: 15 minutes | Cooking time: 30 minutes | Serving: 7

Ingredients

- 1 bacon slice
- Low-sodium Chicken Gravy Mix: 2.8 oz.
- 9 oz. Skinless Chicken Breast, cubed
- Water: 1 cup
- Peas: half cup
- Garlic chopped: half tsp.
- Worcestershire Sauce: 1 tsp.
- Skim milk: 6 oz.
- Sweet Corn: ¼ cup
- 4 Mushrooms, chopped

Directions

1. Add garlic and cut up bacon to a pan, cook for few minutes.
2. Add chicken, Worcestershire sauce and a splash of water. Stir and let it simmer.
3. When chicken is almost cooked, add mushrooms and vegetables.
Cook for few minutes, add milk. Stir well and let it simmer for 20 minutes.
Serve.

Nutrition Per Serving: Kcal 85 | Sodium 237 g | Protein 11.1 g | Carbs 6 g | Fat 1.8 g | Potassium: 411 mg

31. Black Bean & Brown Rice Casserole

Preparation time: 15 minutes | Cooking time: 40 minutes | Serving: 8

Ingredients

- Cumin: half tsp.
- 1/3 cup of dry brown rice
- Boneless & skinless chicken breast: 1 pound, cooked & chopped
- 1 cup of vegetable broth
- Cayenne pepper: ¼ tsp.
- Low fat swiss cheese: 2 cups, shredded
- 1 zucchini, sliced thin
- Olive oil: 1 tbsp.
- 1 can of (4 oz.) Diced green chilies
- Diced onion: 1/3 cup
- Sliced mushrooms: half cup
- 1/3 cup of shredded carrots
- 1 can of (15 oz.) black beans, drained

Directions

1. In a pot, add broth and rice, let it come to a boil. Turn the heat low, simmer for 45 minutes.
2. Let the oven preheat to 350 F. oil spray a baking dish.
3. Saute onion in hot oil until tender. Add chicken, zucchini, seasoning and mushrooms.
4. Cook for few minutes. Transfer to a bowl with cooked rice and chicken mixture, toss with the rest of the ingredients (only half of the swiss cheese).
5. Transfer to the baking dish, top with swiss cheese, cover lightly.
6. Bake for half an hour. Take the foil off, bake for ten minutes more.

Nutrition Per Serving: Kcal 267 | Sodium 237 g | Protein 31 g | Carbs 22 g | Fat 6 g | Potassium: 417 mg

32. Chicken Enchilada Casserole

Preparation time: 15 minutes | Cooking time: 35 minutes | Serving: 6

Ingredients

- 8 corn tortillas of 6"
- Cooked chicken: 2 cups, shredded
- 1 ½ cups of enchilada sauce
- Mexican-blend cheese: 1 cup, low-fat

Directions

1. Let the oven preheat to 350 F. Oil spray a baking dish (2 qt.)
2. Add chicken, half cup of shredded cheese and enchilada sauce (half) to a bowl and toss.
3. Tear the tortillas and cover the baking dish's bottom.
4. Add the chicken mixture on top, add enchilada sauce on top, repeat the layers.
5. Bake for half an hour, covered with foil.
6. Take the foil off, add cheese on top, bake for 5 to 10 minutes.

Nutrition Per Serving: Kcal 230 | Sodium 715 g | Protein 19 g | Carbs 21 g | Fat 7 g | Potassium: 188 mg

33. Stuffed Portobello Mushrooms

Preparation time: 15 minutes | Cooking time: 20 minutes | Serving: 4

Ingredients

- 4 portobello medium mushrooms
- Cooked chicken: 2 cups
- Half red pepper, chopped
- Half red onion, chopped
- 1 egg
- 1/4 cup of breadcrumbs
- Cheddar cheese: 1 cup, shredded
- 2 cloves of minced garlic
- Fresh parsley: 1/4 cup, chopped

Directions

1. Let the oven preheat to 350 F.
2. Take the mushrooms' stem off and clean the mushrooms
3. Toss the gills with the rest of the ingredients. Spoon the mixture into the mushroom caps bake for 18 to 20 minutes.
4. Serve.

Nutrition Per Serving: Kcal 313 | Sodium 380 g | Protein 35 g | Carbs 10 g | Fat 14 g | Potassium: 831 mg

34. Cajun Stuffed Chicken

Preparation time: 15 minutes | Cooking time: 30 minutes | Serving: 4

Ingredients

- Cajun seasoning: 2 tbsp.
- Low-fat pepper jack cheese: 3 oz., shredded
- Bread crumbs: 1 tbsp.
- 1 pound chicken breasts, boneless & skinless
- Frozen spinach: 1 cup, drained

Directions

1. Let the oven preheat to 350 F. Pound the chicken into ¼" of thickness.
2. Add the breadcrumbs and Cajun seasoning to a bowl.
3. Add the rest of the ingredients to a bowl and mix. Place ¼ cup of this mixture onto chicken and roll tightly, secure with toothpicks.
4. Brush the rolls with oil and sprinkle the breadcrumb mixture on top.
5. Line a baking sheet with foil and place the rolls, seam side down.
6. Bake for 35-40 minutes. Slice and serve.
8. Bake for 35 to 40 minutes, or until chicken is cooked through.

Nutrition Per Serving: Kcal 241 | Sodium 380 g | Protein 32 g | Carbs 2 g | Fat 9.7 g | Potassium: 831 mg

35. Pizza Casserole

Preparation time: 15 minutes | Cooking time: 40 minutes | Serving: 8

Ingredients

- Pepperoni: 2 ½ oz.
- Italian Sausage: 2 pounds, without casing
- Italian Seasoning: 1 tsp.
- Olive Oil: 1 tbsp.

- Low-fat Parmesan cheese: 1/4 cup, powdered
- 1 Green Pepper, sliced into small pieces
- Mushrooms: 8 oz., sliced
- Cauliflower florets: 14 oz., into small pieces
- Low-fat Mozzarella cheese: 12 oz., shredded
- Pasta Sauce: 1 ½ cups, low-carb

Directions

1. In a steamer, steam the florets. Pat dry the steamed cauliflower.
2. Let the oven preheat to 400 F.
3. In a pan, cook the sausage for 15 minutes on medium flame. Drain the fat and take it out in a bowl.
4. In the same pan, saute mushrooms in hot oil for 10 minutes, turn the heat off.
5. Oil spray a 13 by 9" baking dish. Add half a cup of sauce and spread.
6. In a bowl, add sausage, green pepper, mushrooms and cauliflower. Toss to combine.
7. Spread half of the mixture on top of the sauce, then add half a cup of the sauce on top.
8. Add half of the pepperoni on top, add mozzarella cheese on top.
9. Layer the rest of the ingredients except for Italian seasoning and parmesan cheese. Mix these two and sprinkle on the top.
10. Bake for half an hour. Serve.

Nutrition Per Serving: Kcal 519 | Sodium 880 g | Protein 27 g | Carbs 7 g | Fat 43 g | Potassium: 500 mg

36. Cheesy Chicken & Broccoli Bake

Preparation time: 15 minutes | Cooking time: 30 minutes | Serving: 2

Ingredients

- Shredded cheese: 1 cup, low-fat
- Frozen cauliflower florets: 2 cups
- Salt, onion powder, pepper & garlic powder: to taste
- Frozen broccoli florets: 1 cup
- Chicken breast: 8 oz., cubed
- Cream of chicken soup: 8 oz., low-fat
- Grated parmesan cheese: half cup

Directions

1. Let the oven preheat to 350 F.
2. Oil spray a skillet and place on medium heat, add chicken and cook completely.
3. Add cauliflower and broccoli to boiling water and boil for 8 to 10 minutes.
4. Drain and mash. Add chicken and soup, mix well.
5. Spoon into a casserole dish, top with cheese.
6. Bake for half an hour at 350 F. serve.

Nutrition Per Serving: Kcal 439 | Sodium 459 g | Protein 21 g | Carbs 8 g | Fat 17 g | Potassium: 454 mg

37. Southwest Chicken with Rice

Preparation time: 15 minutes | Cooking time: 30 minutes | Serving: 6

Ingredients

- Long grain rice: 1 cup
- Ground cumin: 1 tbsp.
- Olive oil: 2 tbsp.
- 4 skinless & boneless chicken breasts
- Chili powder: 2 tbsp.
- Chopped onion: half cup
- 1 cup of jarred red enchilada sauce
- Garlic powder: 1 tsp.
- 1 poblano pepper, chopped
- 1 can of (15 oz.) Roasted diced tomatoes, without liquid
- 1 cup of chicken stock
- 1 cup of corn
- 1 can of (15 oz.) Black beans, drained
- 2 chopped garlic cloves
- Black pepper: ¼ tsp.
- Salt: 1 tsp.

Directions

1. Add garlic powder, chili powder, salt (half tsp.) and cumin to a bowl, and mix.
2. Season the chicken breast with half of the spice mixture.
3. In a pan, add oil on medium flame, cook chicken for 3 to 4 minutes on 1 side. Take it out on a plate.
4. Add more oil to the pan, saute garlic, pepper and onion for 2 to 3 minutes.
5. Add stock, black beans, enchilada sauce, rice, corn, tomatoes and the rest of the spice mixture. Stir and let it come to a simmer.
6. Add chicken back in the pan, cook for 20 minutes, covered.
7. Serve.

Nutrition Per Serving: Kcal 382 | Sodium 924 g | Protein 31 g | Carbs 27 g | Fat 16 g | Potassium: 543 mg

38. Cheesy Crustless Quiche

Preparation time: 15 minutes | Cooking time: 30 minutes | Serving: 8

Ingredients

- Oregano, to season
- Grilled chicken breast: 6 oz., 1" cubes
- 1 cup of skim milk
- Shredded mozzarella cheese: 10 oz., low-fat
- Low fat swiss: 4 oz., cubed
- 3 eggs

Directions

1. Let the oven preheat to 400 F.
2. Oil spray a 9" pie pan.
3. Add the cubed chicken and swiss cheese. Spread the shredded mozzarella on top.
4. Add oregano on top.
5. Whisk eggs with milk and pour over the oregano. Bake for 40 minutes at 400 F.
6. Serve.

Nutrition Per Serving: Kcal 176 | Sodium 435 g | Protein 19.5 g | Carbs 3.6 g | Fat 9 g | Potassium: 501 mg

39. Bacon Cheeseburger Casserole

Preparation time: 15 minutes | Cooking time: 35 minutes | Serving: 10

Ingredients

- 1 tbsp. of avocado oil
- 1 tsp. of garlic powder
- Half tsp. of pepper
- 1 tsp. of onion powder
- bacon: 6 oz.
- 20 oz. of cauliflower rice
- 1 tsp. of parsley
- ⅓ cup of coconut flour
- 1 tsp. of salt
- 1 1/2 pounds of ground beef

Sauce

- 1 tbsp. of coconut flour
- 8 oz. of cheddar cheese
- 1 ½ cups of heavy cream
- 1 tbsp. of butter
- 2 tbsp. of mustard

Directions

1. Let the oven preheat to 400 F.
2. Bake the bacon for 20 minutes in one even layer. Chop the cooked bacon.
3. Add beef to a pan with oil and cook until browned. Add all spices and cook for 1 minute. Take it out in a bowl.
4. Microwave the cauliflower rice for 5 minutes, add salt and coconut flour. Mix well.
5. For the sauce, melt the butter and mix with coconut flour. Turn the heat low, cook for 1 minute, add mustard and heavy cream, and cook until it thickens.
6. In a baking dish (9 by 13"), spread a half cup of sauce, add the cauliflower mixture on top and spread.
7. Add cheddar (4 oz.) over and add beef on top. Add the rest of the sauce on top with cheese.
8. Top with bacon and bake for half an hour, covered with foil.
9. Take the foil off and bake for 5 minutes.

Nutrition Per Serving: Kcal 504 | Sodium 661 g | Protein 21 g | Carbs 7 g | Fat 42 g | Potassium: 423 mg

40. Crockpot Butter Chicken

Preparation time: 15 minutes | Cooking time: 3 hours | Serving: 10

Ingredients

- Carrots or Tomatoes: 8.8 oz.
- Butternut Squash: 21 oz.
- Garlic Puree: 1 tsp.
- Garam Masala: 1 tbsp.
- 3 Chicken Breasts
- 1 Small Onion
- Ginger Puree: 1 tsp.
- Tikka Curry Powder: 1 tsp.
- Chilli Powder: half tsp.
- Turmeric: half tsp.
- Paprika: 1 tsp.
- Salt & Pepper, to taste

Directions

1. Dice the peeled onion, carrots and squash. Transfer to the slow cooker with only 1 tsp. of garam masala. Stir well.
2. Place chicken on top, and sprinkle with the rest of the garam masala.

3. Cook for 3 hours on high. Take the chicken out and cut it into cubes.
4. With a stick blender, mash the vegetable mixture and add the cubed chicken.
5. Mix and serve.

Nutrition Per Serving: Kcal 197 | Sodium 143 g | Protein 26 g | Carbs 16 g | Fat 3 g | Potassium: 904 mg

41. Pulled Barbeque Chicken

Preparation time: 15 minutes | Cooking time: 30 minutes | Serving: 6

Ingredients

- Classic Blend BBQ Sauce: 14 tbsp.
- 4 chicken breast, boneless & skinless
- Dash of salt & pepper

Directions

1. In a pot, add chicken with salt and pepper. Add enough water and boil until cooked completely.
2. Take the chicken out and shred with forks. Transfer to a skillet with BBQ sauce, toss to coat.
3. Serve when heated through.

Nutrition Per Serving: Kcal 85 | Sodium 706 g | Protein 15 g | Carbs 2.3 g | Fat 0.7 g | Potassium: 904 mg

42. Creamy Tuscan Garlic Chicken

Preparation time: 15 minutes | Cooking time: 15 minutes | Serving: 6

Ingredients

- Half cup of parmesan cheese
- Olive oil: 2 tbsp.
- 1 tsp. of garlic powder
- 1 cup of chopped spinach
- 1 cup of heavy cream
- Boneless & skinless chicken breasts: 1½ pounds, sliced thin
- 1 tsp. of Italian seasoning
- Half cup of chicken broth
- Half cup of sun-dried tomatoes

Directions

1. Cook chicken in hot oil for 3 to 5 minutes on each side, take it out on a plate.
2. In the same pan, add the rest of the ingredients except for spinach and tomatoes.
3. Cook until it thickens, add tomatoes and spinach, cook until spinach wilts.
4. Add the chicken back and coat well. Serve.

Nutrition Per Serving: Kcal 365 | Sodium 378 g | Protein 30 g | Carbs 7 g | Fat 25 g | Potassium: 821 mg

43. Garlicky Greek Chicken

Preparation time: 15 minutes | Cooking time: 50 minutes | Serving: 4

Ingredients

- 1 lemon's juice
- Half lb. Of asparagus, trimmed
- 1 lb. Of chicken thighs
- 3 cloves of minced garlic
- Olive oil: 3 tbsp.
- 1 tsp. Of dried oregano
- 1 zucchini, cut into half-moons
- Kosher salt & black pepper
- 1 lemon, sliced

Directions

1. Add oregano, lemon juice, garlic and olive oil (2 tbsp.), mix and add chicken.
2. Coat well keep in the fridge for 15 minutes or 2 hours, covered with plastic wrap.
3. Let the oven preheat to 425 F.
4. Add the rest of the oil to a skillet and heat. Take the chicken out and season with salt and pepper.
5. Place in the pan, cook for 10 minutes, flip and add the lemons, zucchini and asparagus to the skillet.
6. Bake for 15 minutes. Serve.

Nutrition Per Serving: Kcal 315 | Sodium 238 g | Protein 21 g | Carbs 8 g | Fat 17.7 g | Potassium: 456 mg

44. Cilantro Lime Chicken Thighs

Preparation time: 15 minutes | Cooking time: 20 minutes | Serving: 6

Ingredients

- Olive oil: 3 tbsp.
- Chopped fresh cilantro: 1/4 cup
- Ground cumin: 1 tsp.
- Kosher salt: 1 tsp.
- Lime juice: 2 tbsp.
- Lime zest: 1 tbsp.
- 2 pounds chicken thighs, boneless & skinless
- Chili powder: 2 tsp.
- Black pepper: 1 tsp.

Directions

1. Add all the ingredients to a zip lock bag, except for chicken. Mix and add chicken, toss well and keep in the fridge for 2 hours.
2. In a skillet, add olive oil (1 tbsp.) take the chicken out and cook for 4 to 5 minutes on

each side until the internal temperature of the meat reaches 165 F
3. Serve.

Nutrition Per Serving: Kcal 285 | Sodium 218.9 g | Protein 22 g | Carbs 6 g | Fat 8.9 g | Potassium: 400 mg

45. Curried Pork Tenderloin with Apple Cider

Preparation time: 15 minutes | Cooking time: 20 minutes | Serving: 6

Ingredients

- Olive oil: 1 tbsp.
- Cornstarch: 1 tbsp.
- Curry powder: 1 ½ tbsp.
- 1 peeled tart apple, chopped into chunks without seeds
- Pork tenderloin: 16 oz., cut into six pieces
- Chopped onions: 2 cups
- Apple cider: 2 cups

Directions

1. Season the tenderloin with curry powder, let it rest for 15 minutes.
2. Heat oil on medium flame, add tenderloin and cook for 5 to 10 minutes on all sides; take it out on a plate.
3. Saute onion until golden, add apple cider (leaving half cup), turn the heat low, and simmer until reduced by half.
4. Add cornstarch, apple and the rest of the apple cider; cook for 2 minutes until it thickens.
5. Add the pork back to the pan, cook for 5 minutes.
6. Serve with sauce.

Nutrition Per Serving: Kcal 244 | Sodium 48 g | Protein 24 g | Carbs 19 g | Fat 8 g | Potassium: 400 mg

46. Goat Cheese & Spinach Stuffed Chicken Breast

Preparation time: 15 minutes | Cooking time: 30 minutes | Serving: 4

Ingredients

- Olive oil: 2 tbsp.
- Goat cheese: 2 oz.
- Organic spinach: 4 cups
- 4 chicken breasts
- Sliced baby bella mushrooms: 8 oz.
- Garlic powder: half tsp.
- Fresh thyme: 1 tsp.
- 1 sweet onion, sliced
- Salt and pepper

Directions

1. Let the oven preheat to 375 F.
2. Make 6 slits into each chicken breast, do not cut all the way through.
3. Drizzle with oil and season with salt and pepper.
4. In a pan, sauté spinach in oil with garlic powder, cook until it wilts completely.
5. Turn the heat off and mix with goat cheese. Stiff each slit with this mixture.
6. In a pan, heat some oil and saute the rest of the ingredients with salt and pepper. Cook until it caramelizes, and places chicken on top.
7. Bake for 20 to 30 minutes. Serve.

Nutrition Per Serving: Kcal 239 | Sodium 151 g | Protein 28.7 g | Carbs 5.8 g | Fat 12.7 g | Potassium: 356 mg

47. Primavera Stuffed Chicken

Preparation time: 15 minutes | Cooking time: 25 minutes | Serving: 4

Ingredients

- 4 chicken breasts, boneless & skinless
- Italian seasoning: 1 tsp.
- Salt & pepper
- 3 medium tomatoes, half-moons
- Half onion, sliced
- 1 zucchini, cut into half-moons
- Olive oil: 2 tbsp.
- 2 yellow bell peppers, sliced
- Shredded mozzarella: 1 cup

Directions

1. Let the oven preheat to 400 F.
2. In every piece of chicken, make slits and stuff with onion, bell pepper, zucchini and tomatoes.

3. Drizzle with olive oil and sprinkle with salt, pepper and Italian seasoning. Add mozzarella on top.
4. Bake for 25 minutes. Serve.

Nutrition Per Serving: Kcal 245 | Sodium 207 g | Protein 21 g | Carbs 8 g | Fat 11.9 g | Potassium: 361 mg

48. Cajun Chicken and Veggies

Preparation time: 15 minutes | Cooking time: 25 minutes | Serving: 4

Ingredients

- 1 zucchini chopped
- 2 cloves of minced garlic
- Broccoli florets: 2 cups
- 2 to 3 chicken breasts, boneless & skinless: 1" pieces
- Black pepper: ¼ tsp.
- 1 bell pepper, diced
- Olive oil: 2 tbsp.
- Oregano, chili powder, paprika, garlic powder, salt, ground onion: 1 tsp., each

Directions

1. Let the oven preheat to 400 F.
2. In a bowl, add all ingredients toss well and spoon onto 4 foil sheets of 12 by 12".
3. Make into packets by folding and sealing.
4. Bake for 20 to 25 minutes. Serve.

Nutrition Per Serving: Kcal 154 | Sodium 82 g | Protein 21 g | Carbs 5 g | Fat 8 g | Potassium: 427 mg

49. Sweet & Sour Pork

Preparation time: 15 minutes | Cooking time: 40 minutes | Serving: 6

Ingredients

- 1 can of (15 oz.) unsweetened pineapple chunks
- Half cup of water
- 1 tbsp. of light soy sauce
- 1/4 cup of brown sugar (Splenda blend)
- lean pork tenderloin: 1 pound, cut into strips
- 2 tbsp. of corn starch
- 2 sliced green peppers
- Half tsp. of salt
- 1/3 cup of wine vinegar
- 1 small sliced onion, sliced

Directions

1. Cook pork in a nonstick pan until golden brown. Take it out on a plate, drain any fat.
2. Add the rest of the ingredients except for vegetables; only add the liquid from pineapples, mix and add to the same pan. Cook for 2 minutes until it thickens.
3. Add pork back to the pan, cook for half an hour on low.
4. Add vegetables and pineapple, cook for 5 minutes. Serve with rice.

Nutrition Per Serving: Kcal 248 | Sodium 350 g | Protein 18 g | Carbs 36 g | Fat 3.5 g | Potassium: 470 mg

50. Chicken Meatballs & Cauliflower Rice

Preparation time: 15 minutes | Cooking time: 15 minutes | Serving: 6

Ingredients

- 1 tbsp. Of dijon mustard
- Half red onion
- 2 minced garlic cloves
- 1 tbsp. Of olive oil
- 1 pound of ground chicken
- Half tsp. Of black pepper
- ¼ cup of fresh parsley, chopped
- ¾ tsp. Of kosher salt

Sauce

- Chopped fresh parsley: 1¼ cups
- 1 lemon's juice & zest
- 4 scallions, chopped
- Canned coconut milk: 14 oz.
- 1 clove of smashed garlic
- Salt and black pepper

Directions

1. Let the oven preheat to 375 F.
2. Sauté onion in oil for 5 minutes, add garlic and cook for 1 minute. Take it out in a bowl and cool for few minutes.
3. Add the rest of the ingredients, mix and make into balls. Place onto a foil-lined baking sheet.
4. Bake for 17-20 minutes.
5. In a food processor, add the sauce's ingredients. Pulse until smooth.
6. Serve the meatballs with cauliflower rice, topped with sauce.

Nutrition Per Serving: Kcal 205 | Sodium 206 g | Protein 20 g | Carbs 3 g | Fat 13 g | Potassium: 345 mg

51. Greek Lemon Chicken Skewers

Preparation time: 15 minutes | Cooking time: 60 minutes | Serving: 4

Ingredients

- 1 lemon's juice & zest
- 1½ pounds of chicken breast, boneless & skinless, half" strips

- 1 tsp. of dried oregano
- fresh parsley: ¼ cup, chopped
- ¼ cup of Greek yogurt
- 1 tsp. of garlic powder
- Salt and black pepper
- Cayenne pepper, a pinch
- Olive oil, as needed

Directions

1. In a bowl, add all ingredients except for chicken.
2. Mix and add the chicken; coat well. Thread onto skewers.
3. Brush with oil and season with salt and pepper.
4. Cook on a preheated griddle pan for 4-5 minutes on each side.
5. Serve.

Nutrition Per Serving: Kcal 170 | Sodium 116 g | Protein 27 g | Carbs 2 g | Fat 6 g | Potassium: 245 mg

Part 3: Soups & Salads

1. Chicken Taco Soup

Preparation time: 15 minutes | Cooking time: 3-6 hours | Serving: 6

Ingredients

- 1 can of (15 oz.) black beans, drained
- Canned tomatoes & green chilis: 20 oz., diced
- 1 small onion, diced
- Canned tomato sauce: 8 oz.
- 2 chicken breast, skinless &boneless
- Frozen corn: 10 oz.
- Taco seasoning: 1 pack
- 1 can of (15 oz.) Light beans, drained
- Water: half cup
- Chili powder & cumin: 1 tsp., each

Directions

1. In a crockpot, add all the ingredients. Stir and seal the lid.
2. Cook for 3 hours on high or 6 hours on low.
3. Take chicken out and shred finely, put it back in the pot, stir well and serve.

Nutrition Per Serving: Kcal 182 | Sodium 170 mg | Protein 16 g | Carbs 27 g | Fat 1.7 g | Potassium: 647 mg

2. Dill & Caper Egg Salad

Preparation time: 20 minutes | Cooking time: 0 minutes | Serving: 8

Ingredients

- Chopped celery: 3/4 to 1 cup
- Lemon juice: 2 tsp.
- Fresh dill: 1 tbsp., chopped
- Capers: 3 tbsp., drained
- Whole grain mustard: 2 tbsp.
- 8 hard-boiled eggs, yolks & eggs separated
- Sea salt, to taste
- Granulated garlic: ¼ tsp.
- Olive oil: 3 tbsp.
- Black pepper: ¼ tsp.

Directions

1. Chop the egg white and add to a bowl, mix with capers and celery.
2. In a bowl, add egg yolks and mash until smooth. Add lemon juice, oil and mustard; mix. Add more oil if needed to make it creamy.
3. Add the rest of the ingredients, adjust seasoning and fold the caper mixture.
4. Serve and enjoy.

Nutrition Per Serving: Kcal 201 | Sodium 350 mg | Protein 10 g | Carbs 7 g | Fat 15 g | Potassium: 444 mg

3. Butternut Squash Soup

Preparation time: 20 minutes | Cooking time: 30 minutes | Serving: 2

Ingredients

- Half onion, diced
- Garlic: 1 tsp.
- Almond milk soup base: 32 oz.
- Olive oil: 1 tsp.
- Butternut squash: 1 ½ lb.
- Unflavored protein powder: 2 scoops
- Minced ginger: 1 tsp.
- Salt & pepper, to taste

Directions

1. In a pan, sauté onion in hot oil. Add garlic, ginger for 1 minute.
2. Add seasoning, squash, milk base and broth. Stir and let it come to a boil, turn the heat low and simmer for 15 minutes. Make sure squash is tender.
3. Puree with a stick blender, check the temperature of the soup. As it gets under 140 F, add protein powder.
4. Serve.

Nutrition Per Serving: Kcal 195 | Sodium 24.7 mg | Protein 26.8 g | Carbs 18.6 g | Fat 2.6 g | Potassium: 244 mg

4. Good Luck Greens Soup

Preparation time: 10 minutes | Cooking time: 10 minutes | Serving: 6

Ingredients

- Minced garlic: 2 tsp.
- 1 can of (15 oz.) Black eyed peas, rinsed
- 2 onions, chopped
- Swiss chard: 2 bunches, chopped without ribs
- Chicken sausage: 12 oz.
- Salt, paprika, red pepper flakes & garlic powder: ¼ tsp., each
- 1 can of (15 oz.) White beans, rinsed
- 1 bay leaf
- 1 can of (10 oz.) Tomatoes & green chilis, diced
- Chicken broth: 3 to 4 cups
- Onion powder: half tsp.

Directions

1. In an instant pot, add all ingredients stir and cook for 8 minutes.
2. Release steam and serve.

Nutrition Per Serving: Kcal 222 | Sodium 768 mg | Protein 16.2 g | Carbs 18.6 g | Fat 8.1 g | Potassium: 22.7 mg

5. Black Bean & Lentil Soup

Preparation time: 10 minutes | Cooking time: 35 minutes | Serving: 8

Ingredients

- Minced garlic: 2 cloves
- Kosher salt: half tsp.
- 1 yellow onion, small & diced
- 2 small carrots, diced
- Olive oil: 1 tbsp.
- Dried lentils: 1 cup
- Red pepper flakes: half tsp.
- 1 can of (15 oz.) Diced tomatoes
- Vegetable broth: 4 cups
- Chili powder: 1 tsp.
- Cumin: half tsp.
- 1 can of (15 oz.) Black beans, drained
- Black pepper: half tsp.

Directions

1. Saute garlic and in hot oil for 1 minute. Add onion, carrots, cook for 5 minutes.
2. Add the rest of the ingredients, stir well.
3. Let it come to a boil, turn the heat low and simmer for 25-30 minutes, until tender.
4. Serve with grated cheese on top.

Nutrition Per Serving: Kcal 171 | Sodium 640 mg | Protein 10 g | Carbs 29 g | Fat 2 g | Potassium: 510 mg

6. Black & White Bean Greek Salad

Preparation time: 10 minutes | Cooking time: 0 minutes | Serving: 4 to 6

Ingredients

For Salad

- Fresh mint leaves: 1/3 cup, chopped
- Feta cheese: 4 oz., low-fat, crumbled
- Diced red onion: 1/3 cup
- 1 can of (15 oz.) White beans, rinsed
- Diced cucumber: half cup
- 1 can of (15 oz.) Black beans, rinsed

Dressing

- Lemon juice: 3 tbsp.
- Agave nectar: 2 tbsp.
- Oregano leaves: half tsp.
- Olive oil: ¼ cup
- Sea salt & black pepper: half tsp., each
- Garlic powder: half tsp.
- Celery seed: half tsp.

Directions

1. In a bowl, add all ingredients of the dressing. Whisk well.
2. In a bowl, add all ingredients of salad, toss well. Add the dressing on top, toss and keep in the fridge for 1 hour.
3. Serve.

Nutrition Per Serving: Kcal 217 | Sodium 141 mg | Protein 11 g | Carbs 21 g | Fat 4 g | Potassium: 309 mg

7. Golden Red & Orange Bell Pepper Soup

Preparation time: 10 minutes | Cooking time: 30 minutes | Serving: 6

Ingredients

- Half onion, diced
- Fresh marjoram: 3 tsp., chopped
- Salt & pepper, to taste
- 2 carrots, diced
- 8 mixed (yellow & orange) bell peppers, diced
- 1 peeled sweet potato, chopped
- Olive oil: ¼ cup
- 1 celery stalk, chopped
- Vegetable broth: 4 cups

Directions

1. Saute all vegetables (except for potato and bell pepper) in hot oil with salt and pepper. Cook for 4 minutes.

2. Add bell peppers, cook for 6 minutes, add broth and potato.
3. Stir, cover the pot. Let it come to a boil, turn the heat low and simmer for 20 minutes.
4. Puree with a stick blender, adjust consistency and taste.
5. Serve.

Nutrition Per Serving: Kcal 173| Sodium 216.8 mg | Protein 2.2 g | Carbs 21.3 g | Fat 9.8 g | Potassium: 311 mg

8. Garden Salmon Salad

Preparation time: 10 minutes| Cooking time: 0 minutes| Serving: 6

Ingredients

- Fresh peas: 3.5 oz.
- 1 lemon's zest & juice
- 8 radishes, halved
- Mixed seeds: 2 tbsp.
- 2 courgettes
- Rapeseed oil: 3 tbsp.
- 4 skinless salmon fillets: poached, roughly flaked
- Dill: half bunch, fronds picked
- Yogurt: 2 tbsp., low-fat
- Pea shoots: 2.6 oz.

Directions

1. With a peeler, cut the courgettes into long strips, do not use the seedy strips. Add to a bowl, add radishes, peas and ribbons and toss.
2. In a different bowl, whisk the yogurt, juice, zest and oil. Add to the peas bowl, and toss.
3. On a serving platter, add fish and pea shoots.
4. Top with vegetables and add seeds on top.

Nutrition Per Serving: Kcal 434| Sodium 201 mg | Protein 30 g | Carbs 6 g | Fat 31 g | Potassium: 209 mg

9. Avocado Tuna Salad

Preparation time: 10 minutes| Cooking time: 0 minutes| Serving: 2

Ingredients

- 1 avocado
- Lemon zest: 1 tsp.
- Chopped celery: half cup
- Salt & pepper: half tsp., each
- Fresh dill: 2 tbsp., chopped
- 2 pouches yellow fin tuna in olive oil
- Lemon juice: 2 tsp.

Directions

1. In a bowl, add all ingredients, mix with a fork until combined.
2. Keep in the fridge for 1 to 2 hours.
3. Serve.

Nutrition Per Serving: Kcal 368| Sodium 201 mg | Protein 21.6 g | Carbs 13.2 g | Fat 27.5 g | Potassium: 817 mg

10. Mushroom Soup

Preparation time: 10 minutes| Cooking time: 20 minutes| Serving: 4

Ingredients

- 2 onions, chopped
- Chicken stock: 4 cups
- 1 minced garlic clove
- Mushrooms: 17 oz., chopped
- 1 bay leaf
- Butter: 3 oz.
- Low-fat cream: 4 tbsp.
- Plain flour: 2 tbsp.

Directions

1. Saute the garlic and onion in butter for 8 to 10 minutes
2. Add mushrooms, cook for 3 minutes. Add flour and stir well.
3. Add broth, let it come to a boil. Turn the heat low, add bay leaf, and simmer for 10 minutes.
4. Take the bay leaf out, puree with a stick blender, adjust seasoning and serve.

Nutrition Per Serving: Kcal 309| Sodium 217 mg | Protein 11 g | Carbs 14 g | Fat 22 g | Potassium: 345 mg

11. Ground Beef Veggie Stew

Preparation time: 10 minutes | Cooking time: 30 minutes | Serving: 6

Ingredients

- Olive oil: 1 tbsp.
- Lean ground beef: 1 pound
- 2 cans of (15 oz.) Diced tomatoes
- 1 small zucchini, diced
- 1 summer squash, diced
- Fresh cilantro: 3 tbsp., chopped
- 1 cup of water
- Salt: 1 tsp.
- 1 red bell pepper, chopped
- Pepper, to taste

Directions

1. Cook beef in a pan for 5 to 7 minutes, drain.
2. In a pan, saute bell pepper, squash and zucchini in hot oil for 5 to 7 minutes.
3. Add the rest of the ingredients with the beef. Stir well, let it come to a boil, turn the heat low and simmer for 5 to 7 minutes.
4. Serve with cilantro on top.

Nutrition Per Serving: Kcal 180 | Sodium 663 mg | Protein 16 g | Carbs 9 g | Fat 9 g | Potassium: 351 mg

12. Broccoli Cheese Soup

Preparation time: 10 minutes | Cooking time: 30 minutes | Serving: 8

Ingredients

- 4 Cups of Broccoli florets
- Onion powder: half tsp.
- Shredded carrots: half cup
- 4 Cups of Chicken broth
- Garlic powder: half tsp.
- salt & pepper, to taste
- Shredded cheddar: 4 cups, low-fat
- 1 Cup of Heavy low-fat cream
- Cream cheese: 4 oz.

Directions

1. In a pot, add carrots, florets and broth.
2. Let it come to a boil, turn the heat low and simmer for 6 to 8 minutes.
3. Add onion and garlic powder. Cool the soup to 150 F, then add cheese keep mixing.
4. Add cream and turn the heat off; adjust seasoning.
5. Serve.

Nutrition Per Serving: Kcal 346 | Sodium 564 mg | Protein 14 g | Carbs 8 g | Fat 30 g | Potassium: 403 mg

13. Best Chili

Preparation time: 10 minutes | Cooking time: 30 minutes | Serving: 6

Ingredients

- Half sweet onion, chopped
- 2 celery stalks, diced
- Dried oregano: 2 tsp.
- 3 minced cloves of garlic
- Chili powder: 2tbsp.
- 3 slices of bacon, half-inch strips
- 2 bell peppers, chopped
- Ground lean beef: 2 lb.
- 1 can of (28 oz.) Fire-roasted tomatoes
- Salt & pepper, to taste
- Smoked paprika: 2 tbsp.
- Ground cumin: 2 tsp.
- Chicken broth: 2 cups, low-sodium

Directions

1. Cook bacon until crispy. Take it out on a plate.
2. Add peppers, onion and celery to the pan cook for 6 minutes.
3. Add garlic, cook for 60 seconds. Add beef on one side, cook until not pink anymore. Drain any fat.
4. Addd spices and cook for 2 minutes.
5. Add broth, tomatoes and simmer for 10-15 minutes.
6. Serve with bacon, avocado and jalapenos on top.

Nutrition Per Serving: Kcal 356 | Sodium 555 mg | Protein 27 g | Carbs 4 g | Fat 17.8 g | Potassium: 400 mg

14. Cauliflower Soup

Preparation time: 10 minutes | Cooking time: 30 minutes | Serving: 6

Ingredients

- Ground cumin: half tbsp.
- 1 minced garlic clove
- 1 cauliflower head: 52 oz., broken into florets
- Chicken stock: 25 oz.
- 4 thyme sprigs
- Olive oil: 2 tbsp.
- 1 onion, diced
- Half bunch parsley, chopped
- 1 celery stick, diced
- Low-fat cream: 3.3 oz.

Directions

1. Let the oven preheat to 420 F.

2. Toss the florets with oil (1 tbsp.), thyme and cumin. Spread on a baking sheet, roast for 15 minutes. Take the thyme out later.
3. In a pan, saute celery and onion in hot oil for 10 minutes. Add garlic and cook for 1 minute.
4. Add florets and add broth, simmer for 10 minutes. Pulse with a stick blender, adjust seasoning and serve with a drizzle of olive oil.

Nutrition Per Serving: Kcal 176 | Sodium 275 mg | Protein 8 g | Carbs 14 g | Fat 8 g | Potassium: 300 mg

15. Easy Pork Posole

Preparation time: 10 minutes | Cooking time: 6 hours | Serving: 8

Ingredients

- Boneless pork shoulder: half pound (butt roast), cubed
- Canola oil: 1 tbsp.
- 2 tomatoes, chopped without seeds
- 1 jalapeno pepper, chopped without seeds
- Chicken broth: 6 cups
- 1 can of (16 oz.) Hominy, drained
- 4 scallions, chopped
- Andouille sausage links: half pound, cooked & sliced
- Chili powder: 1 tbsp.
- 1 onion, diced
- Ground cumin: 1 tsp.
- Fresh cilantro: 1 cup, chopped
- Cayenne pepper: half tsp.
- 2 minced garlic cloves
- Coarsely black pepper: half tsp.

Directions

1. Cook pork and sausage in hot oil over medium flame. Drain and add to a slow cooker (4 qt.)
2. Add the rest of the ingredients, stir well.
3. Cook for 6 to 8 hours on low, covered. Serve as it is or Serve in tortillas with desired toppings.

Nutrition Per Serving: Kcal 190 | Sodium 780 mg | Protein 14 g | Carbs 12 g | Fat 11 g | Potassium: 307 mg

16. Creamy Chicken Soup

Preparation time: 10 minutes | Cooking time: 20 minutes | Serving: 6

Ingredients

- Chicken broth: 4 cups
- Half onion, chopped
- Dried dill: ¼ tsp.
- 2 minced cloves of garlic
- 2 chicken breasts, boneless & skinless
- Dried thyme: half tsp.
- Diced celery: half cup
- Low-fat heavy cream: ¾ cup
- Broccoli florets: 1 ½ cups
- Diced carrots: 1 cup
- Cream cheese: 4 oz.

Directions

1. In an instant pot, add all ingredients (except for cream cheese & cheese) and stir.
2. Cook for ten minutes on high pressure. Release pressure.
3. Take the chicken out and shred, add back to the pot.
4. Again seal the lid and select time to 0. Do a quick release, add cream cheese and cream. Stir, adjust seasoning and serve.

Nutrition Per Serving: Kcal 285 | Sodium 333 mg | Protein 19 g | Carbs 6 g | Fat 19 g | Potassium: 367 mg

17. Acorn Squash Soup

Preparation time: 10 minutes | Cooking time: 50 minutes | Serving: 6

Ingredients

- Olive oil: 3 tbsp.
- 4 minced cloves of garlic
- 4 cups of chicken broth
- Salt and pepper
- 2 acorn squash
- Shredded parmesan: half cup
- Cayenne pepper: ¼ tsp.
- Cream: half cup, low-fat
- Dried sage: half tsp.

Directions

1. With a fork, pierce the squash all over and microwave for 10 minutes on high.

2. Let the oven preheat to 400 F. slice the squash in half, take the middle part out, drizzle with oil, and season with salt, garlic, and pepper.
3. Place on a baking sheet, round side down. Roast for half an hour.
4. Take it out and let it cool slightly; spoon the flesh in a Dutch oven.
5. Add broth, sage and cayenne, stir and blend with a stick blender.
6. Add cream, adjust seasoning. Cook until heated through.
7. Serve.

Nutrition Per Serving: Kcal 222| Sodium 367 mg | Protein 5 g | Carbs 16 g | Fat 14 g | Potassium: 365 mg

18. Red Pepper, Squash & Harissa Soup

Preparation time: 10 minutes| Cooking time: 60 minutes| Serving: 6

Ingredients

- 2 red bell pepper, chopped
- Chikecn stock: 5 cups
- 2 red onion, chopped
- Ground coriander: 1 tbsp.
- Rapeseed oil: 3 tbsp.
- 1 butternut squash: 21 oz., peeled & chunks
- 3 garlic cloves, unpeeled
- Harissa paste: 2 tbsp.
- Ground cumin: 2 tsp.
- Low-fat double cream: 1.6 oz.

Directions

1. Let the oven preheat to 350 F.
2. Toss the vegetables with oil, seasoning and unpeeled garlic cloves
3. Spread on a baking sheet, roast for 45 minutes, stir the tray after half an hour.
4. Squeeze the garlic and transfer everything to a pot; add the rest of the ingredients.
5. Let it simmer for few minutes, puree with a stick blender. Adjust seasoning and serve.

Nutrition Per Serving: Kcal 205| Sodium 365 mg | Protein 9 g | Carbs 15 g | Fat 11 g | Potassium: 278 mg

19. Mexican Cabbage Roll Soup

Preparation time: 10 minutes| Cooking time: 30 minutes| Serving: 6

Ingredients

- Salt: half tsp.
- 1 can of (~15 oz.) Beef broth
- 1 onion, chopped
- Garlic powder: 3/4 tsp.
- 3 cans of (4 oz., each) chopped green chiles
- Lean ground beef: 1 pound
- 6 cups of chopped cabbage
- Pepper: ¼ tsp.
- 2 cups of water
- Olive oil: 1 tbsp.
- Chopped cilantro: 2 tbsp.

Directions

1. In a pan, add beef and seasoning for 5 to 7 minutes on medium flame.
2. Take it out in a bowl.
3. Saute cabbage and onion in hot oil for 4 to 6 minutes.
4. Add broth, beef, chiles and water. Stir, let it come to a boil, turn the heat low and simmer for 10 minutes.
5. Add cilantro and serve.

Nutrition Per Serving: Kcal 186| Sodium 604 mg | Protein 17 g | Carbs 10 g | Fat 9 g | Potassium: 278 mg

20. Zuppa Toscana Soup

Preparation time: 10 minutes| Cooking time: 30 minutes| Serving: 6

Ingredients

- 3 minced cloves garlic
- 1 onion, diced
- Chopped kale: 2 cups
- 1 head of cauliflower, chopped
- Ground turkey sausage: 1 lb.
- 4 slices of bacon, diced
- Heavy cream: ¾ cup
- Kosher salt, to taste
- Chicken broth: 6 cups, low-sodium
- Black pepper: half tsp.

Directions

1. Cook bacon until crispy and take it out on a plate.
2. In the bacon fat, saute onion, garlic for 5 minutes.
3. Add sausage and cook for 5 minutes.
4. Add the rest of the ingredients, cook for ten minutes.
5. Serve with crispy bacon on top.

Nutrition Per Serving: Kcal 260| Sodium 404 mg | Protein 19 g | Carbs 9 g | Fat 18 g | Potassium: 312 mg

21. Rainbow Power Salad with Roasted Chickpeas

Preparation time: 15 minutes | Cooking time: 40 minutes | Serving: 2 to 4

Ingredients

- 1 zucchini
- Olive oil: 1 tbsp.
- Fresh basil: ¼ cup, sliced
- 3 tri-color carrots
- 1 can of chickpeas, rinsed
- Salt and pepper
- Chili powder: 1 tsp.
- Cumin: half tsp.

Directions

1. Let the oven preheat to 400 F.
2. Pat dry the chickpeas and toss with salt, pepper, chili powder, cumin and oil.
3. Spread on a baking sheet and bake for 30 to 40 minutes, shaking the tray once.
4. Cut the carrots into thin ribbons with a peeler. Spiralizer the zucchini and pat dry.
5. Toss the carrots and zucchini with basil.
6. Serve with your desired dressing on top.

Nutrition Per Serving: Kcal 290 | Sodium 686 mg | Protein 11.7 g | Carbs 38 g | Fat 11.7 g | Potassium: 665 mg

22. Carne Asada Steak Salad

Preparation time: 15 minutes | Cooking time: 10 minutes | Serving: 4

Ingredients

- Sirloin steak: 1 lb.
- Half avocado, diced
- Baby spinach: 8 oz., fresh
- Low-fat dressing: 4 to 8 tbsp.
- 1 yellow bell pepper, chopped
- Carne Asada seasoning: 1 ½ oz.
- 10 to 15 cherry tomatoes, cut in half

Directions

1. Season the steak with Asada seasoning and keep it in the fridge for 20 to 30 minutes.
2. Oil spray a skillet and cook steak for 3 minutes on each side.
3. Cut it against the grain.
4. In a bowl, add the rest of the ingredients, toss and serve with steak on top.

Nutrition Per Serving: Kcal 240 | Sodium 214 mg | Protein 28 g | Carbs 10 g | Fat 11 g | Potassium: 888 mg

23. Healthy Grilled Chicken Salad

Preparation time: 15 minutes | Cooking time: 0 minutes | Serving: 2

Ingredients

- Chopped scallions: 2 tbsp.
- Grilled chicken breast: 1 cup, diced
- Dijon mustard: 1 tsp.
- Diced celery: ¼ cup
- Black pepper, to taste
- Light mayonnaise: 1 tbsp.
- Half lemon's juice

Directions

1. In a bowl, toss all ingredients. Serve with crackers.

Nutrition Per Serving: Kcal 150 | Sodium 170 mg | Protein 22 g | Carbs 3 g | Fat 5 g | Potassium: 888 mg

24. Grilled Steak Salad

Preparation time: 15 minutes | Cooking time: 10 minutes | Serving: 2

Ingredients

- 4 flat-iron steaks, 4 oz., each
- 2 lemons, cut in half
- Lemon juice: 1 tbsp.
- Fresh chives: 1 tbsp., chopped
- Olive oil: 1 tbsp.
- Parmigiano-reggiano cheese: ¼ cup, shaved
- Dijon mustard: half tsp.
- Kosher salt & black pepper
- Fresh thyme: 1 tsp., chopped
- Baby arugula: 4 cups

Directions

1. Season the steak with thyme, salt and pepper. Cook steaks for 4 minutes on one side.
2. Take it out on a plate, add lemons to the pan, cook round side up for 3 minutes.
3. Slice the steak against the grain.
4. Add the rest of the ingredients to a bowl, except for cheese and arugula. Whisk well and add arugula, toss to coat.
5. Serve the salad with sliced steak and cheese, lemon on top.

Nutrition Per Serving: Kcal 258 | Sodium 360 mg | Protein 25 g | Carbs 4 g | Fat 16 g | Potassium: 458 mg

25. Buttermilk Chicken with Chopped Salad

Preparation time: 15 minutes | Cooking time: 20 minutes | Serving: 6

Ingredients

- Fresh thyme: 1 tbsp.
- Boneless skinless chicken thighs: 1 1/2 lbs., half-inch pieces
- 1 lemon's juice
- 1 cucumber, diced
- Salt & pepper
- Low-fat buttermilk: 2/3 cup
- Red grapes: 1 cup, halved
- 1 head of butterleaf lettuce
- Chopped red onion: 1/4 cup

Directions

1. Place a grill pan on medium heat.
2. In a bowl, add milk, zest, lemon juice, thyme, salt and pepper. Mix and add the chicken; coat well.
3. Grill chicken for ten minutes on 1 side. Take it out on a plate and slice.
4. Add the rest of the ingredients to a bowl, toss and serve with chicken on top.
5. With desired dressing.

Nutrition Per Serving: Kcal 165 | Sodium 236 mg | Protein 25 g | Carbs 7 g | Fat 4 g | Potassium: 722 mg

26. Herbed Shrimp with Tomato-Spinach Salad

Preparation time: 15 minutes | Cooking time: 10 minutes | Serving: 4

Ingredients

- Fresh oregano: 2 tbsp., chopped
- Honey: half tsp.
- Olive oil: 2 tbsp.
- Fresh flat-leaf parsley: ¼ cup, chopped
- Red wine vinegar: 2 tbsp.
- Black pepper & kosher salt: half tsp., each
- Low-fat feta cheese: 2 oz., crumbled
- Grape tomatoes: 1 cup, halved
- Fennel bulb: half cup, sliced
- Baby spinach: 4 cups
- Mint leaves: ¼ cup
- Large shrimp: 1 pound, peeled & deveined
- Radicchio: half cup, sliced

Directions

1. In a food processor, add the first 6 ingredients, pulse until chopped.
2. In a bowl, add shrimp and parsley mixture (1 ½ tbsp.) coat well.
3. In a bowl, add tomatoes and the rest of the parsley mixture, toss well.
4. Oil spray a grill pan and heat it. Cook shrimp for 3 minutes, flip and cook for 1 minute.
5. To the tomatoes, add the rest of the vegetables. Serve with shrimps & cheese on top.

Nutrition Per Serving: Kcal 212 | Sodium 616 mg | Protein 25 g | Carbs 8 g | Fat 11.4 g | Potassium: 421 mg

27. Sauteed Brussel Sprout Salad

Preparation time: 15 minutes | Cooking time: 20 minutes | Serving: 4

Ingredients

- Salt and pepper: ¼ tsp., each
- Olive oil: 2 tsp.
- Shredded brussels sprouts: 3 cups
- 6 strips of turkey bacon, chopped

Directions

1. Cook turkey bacon until crispy. Add the rest of the ingredients.
2. Toss and cook for 8 minutes and serve.

Nutrition Per Serving: Kcal 113 | Sodium 196 mg | Protein 7 g | Carbs 6 g | Fat 7 g | Potassium: 263 mg

28. Chicken, Red Potato & Green Bean Salad

Preparation time: 15 minutes | Cooking time: 20 minutes | Serving: 4

Ingredients

Dressing

- Red wine vinegar: 3 tbsp.
- Salt: half tsp.
- Fresh parsley: 1/3 cup, chopped
- Lemon juice: 1 tbsp.
- Grainy dijon mustard: 1 tbsp.
- 1 minced garlic clove
- Olive oil: 1 tbsp.
- Black pepper: ¼ tsp.

For salad

- Salt: 1 tsp.
- Chopped red onion: 2 tbsp.
- Green beans: half pound
- Small red potatoes: 1 pound
- Salad greens: 6 cups
- Cooked chicken cubed: 2 cups

Directions

1. In a bowl, add all ingredients of dressing whisk well.
2. In a pot, add salt and potatoes, enough water to cover them. Simmer for ten minutes.
3. Add beans and simmer for 4 minutes more. Drain and wash with tap water.

4. Cut the boiled potatoes into 4 parts.
5. In a bowl, add all the ingredients, pour dressing on top.
6. Toss and serve.

Nutrition Per Serving: Kcal 269 | Sodium 761 mg | Protein 22.4 g | Carbs 26 g | Fat 8.8 g | Potassium: 271 mg

29. Club Salad with Pulled Chicken

Preparation time: 15 minutes | Cooking time: 3-6 hours | Serving: 4

Ingredients

For Chicken

- Chicken broth: half cup
- 1 lb. Chicken breasts, boneless & skinless
- Salt and pepper: ¼ tsp., each
- Light italian dressing: 2 tbsp.

For salad

- Cherry tomatoes: 1 cup, halved
- 3 boiled eggs, cut into fours
- 4 strips of turkey bacon, cooked
- Romaine lettuce: 4 cups, torn
- Fat free creamy dressing, as needed
- 1 avocado, diced

Directions

1. Season the chicken with salt and pepper.
2. Place in a slow cooker and pour Italian dressing on top with broth.
3. Cook for 3 hours on high or 6 hours on low.
4. Take it out and shred.
5. In a bowl, add the salad ingredients, add shredded chicken. Toss and serve.

Nutrition Per Serving: Kcal 288 | Sodium 331 mg | Protein 333 g | Carbs 10 g | Fat 14 g | Potassium: 391 mg

30. Grilled Chicken & Wheat-Berry Salad

Preparation time: 15 minutes | Cooking time: 2 hours & 10 minutes | Serving: 16

Ingredients

- 1 cup of hard winter wheat berries, rinsed well
- Peeled green apple: 1 cup, cut into strips
- 1 bay leaf
- 4 cups of water
- Chopped red bell pepper: half cup
- Salt & black pepper: ¼ tsp., each
- Dijon mustard: 2 tsp.
- 2 cups of baby spinach
- Chopped scallions: ¼ cup
- 4 chicken breasts, skinless & boneless

Directions

1. In a pan, add water, berries and bay leaf. Cook, covered for 2 hours on medium flame.
2. Add chopped spinach, wheat berries, bell pepper, apple, mustard and dressing, and toss in a bowl.
3. Season the chicken with salt and pepper, grill the chicken for 5 minutes on each side. Slice it.
4. Serve the wheat berry salad with chicken & scallions on top.

Nutrition Per Serving: Kcal 332 | Sodium 432 mg | Protein 29 g | Carbs 30 g | Fat 12 g | Potassium: 381 mg

31. Balsamic Watermelon Chicken Salad

Preparation time: 10 minutes | Cooking time: 30 minutes | Serving: 4

Ingredients

- 1 lb. of chicken breasts, boneless skinless
- Baby spinach: 4 cups
- Cubed watermelon: 2 cups
- All purpose seasoning: 3 tbsp.
- 1 cup of balsamic vinegar
- Blue cheese: half cup, crumbled
- Olive oil: 1 tbsp.
- Sliced almonds: ¼ cup

Directions

1. In a pan, add balsamic vinegar and let it come to a boil.
2. Turn the heat low and simmer for 15 to 20 minutes.
3. Season the chicken with seasoning and drizzle with oil.
4. Grill until cooked and cube it.
5. In a bowl, add all ingredients toss well. Serve

Nutrition Per Serving: Kcal 317 | Sodium 283 mg | Protein 30 g | Carbs 19 g | Fat 11.7 g | Potassium: 750 mg

Part 4: Fish & Seafood Recipes

Tuna Patties

Preparation time: 15 minutes | Cooking time: 30 minutes | Serving: 9

Ingredients

- Scallions, chopped
- 3 eggs
- 4 cans of (5 oz.) Tuna in water
- Grated Parmesan cheese: 1 cup, low-fat

Directions

1. In a bowl, add all ingredients and mix.
2. Make into 9 patties, place on a parchment-lined baking sheet.
3. Bake for 25 to 30 minutes at 350 F.
4. Serve.

Nutrition Per Serving: Kcal 85 | Sodium 171 mg | Protein 7.8 g | Carbs 1.8 g | Fat 5.2 g | Potassium: 311 mg

2. Shrimp & Sausage Cajun Pasta

Preparation time: 15 minutes | Cooking time: 20 minutes | Serving: 4-6

Ingredients

- Half lb. Shrimp: cooked, peeled & deveined
- Andouille sausage: 8 oz., sliced
- Tomato paste: 1 tbsp.
- Cajun seasoning: 1 to 2 tsp., salt-free
- 1 tomato, diced without seeds
- Salt & pepper, to taste
- Butternut squash noodles: 12 oz.
- 1 jalapeno pepper, sliced without seeds

Directions

1. Oil spray a pan and cook sausage until browned.
2. Add shrimps until pink. Take it out in a bowl.
3. Oil spray the pan again and saute onion until tender. Add tomatoes and cook for 2 minutes.
4. Add water (~1/4 cup) and tomato paste with seasoning, stir and cook for 2 to 3 minutes.
5. Add squash noodles and cook for ten minutes. Add the cooked sausage mixture and cook for 5 minutes.
6. Serve with jalapenos on top.

Nutrition Per Serving: Kcal 216 | Sodium 276 mg | Protein 18 g | Carbs 4 g | Fat 5 g | Potassium: 301 mg

3. Mustard Crusted Salmon

Preparation time: 15 minutes | Cooking time: 10 minutes | Serving: 2

Ingredients

- Dijon mustard: 1 ½ tbsp.
- Cayenne pepper: 1/8 tsp.
- Granulated garlic: half tsp.
- Wild caught salmon: 8 oz.
- Dried parsley, kosher salt & black pepper: ¼ tsp., each

Directions

1. Let the oven preheat to 400 F.
2. Cut the salmon into 2 portions. Spread mustard all over the salmon.
3. Season the fish and oil spray it.
4. Cook in a non-stick pan on medium heat for 2 minutes on each side.
5. Flip after oil spray the salmon. Place the pan in the oven and bake for 3 minutes at 400 F, until the internal temperature reaches 145 F.
6. Serve.

Nutrition Per Serving: Kcal 198 | Sodium 276 mg | Protein 28 g | Carbs 0 g | Fat 7 g | Potassium: 301 mg

4. Garlic Shrimp & Veggie Foil Packs

Preparation time: 15 minutes | Cooking time: 20 minutes | Serving: 4

Ingredients

- Chopped zucchini: 3 to 4 cups
- Olive oil: 3 tbsp.
- 4 minced garlic cloves
- Large shrimp: 1 pound, peeled & deveined

- Salt & pepper, to taste
- Minced cilantro: 2 tbsp.
- Paprika: 1 tsp.

Directions

1. In a bowl, add all ingredients. Toss to combined.
2. Tear 18 by 12" pieces of foil and place the equal mixture in each foil. Fold the packet.
3. Bake for 15 to 20 minutes at 400 F.
4. Serve.

Nutrition Per Serving: Kcal 227 | Sodium 765 mg | Protein 24 g | Carbs 4 g | Fat 12 g | Potassium: 356 mg

5. Tilapia Piccata

Preparation time: 15 minutes | Cooking time: 10 minutes | Serving: 2

Ingredients

- 2 tilapia filets
- Butter: half tbsp.
- Salt & pepper, to taste
- Olive oil: 1 tbsp.
- All-purpose flour: 1 tbsp.
- Minced garlic: 1 tsp.
- Capers: 1 tbsp.
- Champagne vinegar: ¼ cup
- 1 lemon's juice

Directions

1. Oil spray a hot pan.
2. Season the tilapia with salt, pepper and place in the pan.
3. Cook for 2 minutes on one side. Take it out on a plate.
4. Add butter to the pan, whisk in flour and cook until it thickens.
5. Add vinegar and lemon juice, keep whisking for 2 to 3 minutes.
6. Add capers and cook for 1 minute. Adjust seasoning to your taste.
7. Serve the fish with sauce.

Nutrition Per Serving: Kcal 222 | Sodium 323 mg | Protein 14 g | Carbs 4.4 g | Fat 7 g | Potassium: 312 mg

6. Easy Fish Tacos

Preparation time: 15 minutes | Cooking time: 10 minutes | Serving: 8

Ingredients

For Baja Sauce

- Low-fat Greek yogurt: ¼ cup
- Shredded cabbage: 2 cups
- Cumin: ¼ tsp.
- 1 tomato, diced
- Low-fat cottage cheese: ¼ cup
- Half a lime's juice

For tacos

- 10 Corn tortillas
- Olive oil: 1 tsp.
- Shrimp: 1 lb., peeled & deveined, without tails
- Cumin: half tsp.
- Chopped cilantro & scallion (garnish)

Directions

1. In a bowl, add all ingredients of sauce, mix well.
2. In a bowl, toss shrimps with cumin and oil. Cook shrimps on a medium flame for 5 to 10 minutes. Turn the heat off.
3. Add shrimps in the warmed tortillas, add sauce, scallions & cilantro on top.
4. Serve.

Nutrition Per Serving: Kcal 138 | Sodium 192 mg | Protein 15 g | Carbs 16.2 g | Fat 2.2 g | Potassium: 323 mg

7. Veggie Bowls With Smoked Salmon

Preparation time: 15 minutes | Cooking time: 10 minutes | Serving: 2

Ingredients

- 1 chopped cucumber
- Shredded carrots: half cup
- Salad dressing, as needed
- 1 chopped red bell pepper
- Green giant riced vegetables: 2 packs
- Red cabbage: 1 cup, shredded
- Smoked salmon: 1 cup, flaked

Directions

1. Let the oven preheat to 425 F. Oil spray a baking sheet and spread the riced vegetables on the sheet.
2. Bake for 5 to 7 minutes, stirring as needed.
3. In 2 serving bowls, add the riced vegetables.
4. Add the rest of the ingredients on top. Toss and serve.

Nutrition Per Serving: Kcal 204 | Sodium 181 mg | Protein 13 g | Carbs 12 g | Fat 2 g | Potassium: 320 mg

8. Sheet Pan Baked Tilapia

Preparation time: 15 minutes | Cooking time: 15 minutes | Serving: 4

Ingredients

- Broccoli florets: 3 cups, diced
- Minced garlic: 1 tbsp.
- Red pepper flakes: ¼ tsp.

- Sliced carrots: 1 1/2 cups
- 4 tilapia fillets
- Olive oil: 4 tbsp.
- 1 sliced yellow squash
- Salt & pepper
- Fresh parsley: 1 tbsp., chopped
- Onion powder: ¼ tsp.

Directions

1. Let the oven preheat to 400 F.
2. Toss the vegetables with olive oil (2 tbsp.) and season with salt, pepper and spread on a baking sheet.
3. Add the rest of the oil to the same bowl and mix with the rest of the ingredients. Coat well and season the fish with salt and pepper.
4. Place on the same baking sheet, bake for 12 to 15 minutes.
5. Serve.

Nutrition Per Serving: Kcal 343 | Sodium 148 mg | Protein 37 g | Carbs 12 g | Fat 17 g | Potassium: 1011 mg

9. BBQ Roasted Salmon

Preparation time: 15 minutes | Cooking time: 15 minutes | Serving: 4

Ingredients

- Lemon juice: 2 tbsp.
- Ground cumin: ¾ tsp.
- Pineapple juice: ¼ cup
- Brown sugar: 2 tbsp.
- Chili powder: 4 tsp.
- Lemon zest: 2 tsp.
- Salt: half tsp.
- 4 salmon fillets
- Cinnamon: ¼ tsp.

Directions

1. Let the oven preheat to 400 F.
2. In a bowl, add lemon and pineapple juice mixture and add fish. Coat well.
3. Keep in the fridge for 1 hour, flipping often. Drain and discard the liquid.
4. Add the rest of the ingredients to a bowl and mix. Season the fish with this mixture.
5. Oil spray a baking sheet and bake the salmon on top for 12-15 minutes.

Nutrition Per Serving: Kcal 225 | Sodium 407 mg | Protein 34 g | Carbs 7 g | Fat 6 g | Potassium: 356 mg

10. Broiled Tilapia Parmesan

Preparation time: 15 minutes | Cooking time: 10 minutes | Serving: 8

Ingredients

- Softened butter: ¼ cup
- Black pepper: ¼ tsp.
- Light mayonnaise: 3 tbsp.
- Low-fat parmesan cheese: half cup
- Tilapia fillets: 2 pounds
- Lemon juice: 2 tbsp.
- Dried basil: ¼ tsp.
- Onion powder & celery salt: 1/8 tsp., each

Directions

1. Let the broiler preheat. Oil spray a broiling pan.
2. In a bowl, add all the ingredients except for fish.
3. Place fish on the prepared sheet and broil for 2-3 minutes, few inches away.
4. Flip and broil for 2 minutes more. Take the fish out and top with the mixture
5. Broil for 2 minutes more, serve.

Nutrition Per Serving: Kcal 224 | Sodium 220.5 mg | Protein 24 g | Carbs 0.8 g | Fat 13 g | Potassium: 356 mg

11. Halibut with Cilantro, Lime & Garlic

Preparation time: 15 minutes | Cooking time: 15 minutes | Serving: 3

Ingredients

- White wine: half cup
- Minced garlic: 2 tsp.
- Fresh cilantro: ¼ cup, chopped
- 3 halibut fillets of 4 oz. Each
- 1 lime's juice
- Olive oil: 1 tbsp.

Directions

1. Let the oven preheat to 400 F. oil spray a 9 by 13" baking pan.
2. In a bowl, add all the ingredients except for fish, mix well.
3. Place the fish in the prepared baking dish, pour the mixture over.
4. Bake for 12-15 minutes. Serve.

Nutrition Per Serving: Kcal 177 | Sodium 80 mg | Protein 21 g | Carbs 1 g | Fat 6 g | Potassium: 316 mg

12. Oven Fried Fish

Preparation time: 15 minutes | Cooking time: 20 minutes | Serving: 4

Ingredients

- Ground golden flax: half cup
- Sea salt: half tsp.
- Baking powder: ¼ tsp.
- Ground almonds: half cup
- Paprika: 1 tsp.
- Garlic powder & dried onion powder: half tsp., each
- White fish fillet: 1 pound
- Grated parmesan: ¼ cup, low-fat
- 2 eggs

Directions

1. Let the oven preheat to 430 F with some butter in a pan.
2. In a bowl, whisk the eggs.
3. In a different bowl, add the rest of the ingredients except for fish.
4. Coat the fish in the breading, then in eggs, again in the breading.
5. Place in the melted butter pan, bake for ten minutes. Oil spray the fish and flip.
6. Bake for 5 to 10 minutes more. Broil for 2 minutes.
7. Serve.

Nutrition Per Serving: Kcal 464 | Sodium 611 mg | Protein 35 g | Carbs 10 g | Fat 33 g | Potassium: 555 mg

13. Low Carb Baked Fish

Preparation time: 15 minutes | Cooking time: 25 minutes | Serving: 5

Ingredients

- Salt and pepper, to taste
- Fish fillets: 15 oz.
- Seafood seasoning: 1 ½ tsp.
- Paprika, to taste

Directions

1. Let the oven preheat to 375 F.
2. Place fish on a parchment-lined baking sheet. Season with the seasoning.
3. Bake for 25 minutes.

Nutrition Per Serving: Kcal 82 | Sodium 44 mg | Protein 17 g | Carbs 0 g | Fat 9 g | Potassium: 256 mg

14. Salmon With Green Beans

Preparation time: 15 minutes | Cooking time: 10 minutes | Serving: 2

Ingredients

- Non-dairy butter: 3 oz.
- Salt & pepper, to taste
- Green beans: 9 oz. Rinsed & trimmed
- Salmon: 12 oz., boneless fillets
- Half lemon's juice

Directions

1. In a large pan, melt butter and add vegetables and fish.
2. Cook salmon for 3 to 4 minutes on 1 side, saute green beans.
3. Sprinkle with salt and pepper.
4. Serve the dish with lemon juice on top.

Nutrition Per Serving: Kcal 70 | Sodium 44 mg | Protein 21 g | Carbs 3 g | Fat 14 g | Potassium: 301 mg

15. Baked Cod with Goat's Cheese & Thyme

Preparation time: 10 minutes | Cooking time: 12 minutes | Serving: 2

Ingredients

- 2 cod fillets: 4 oz., each
- 1 grated garlic clove
- 2 tomatoes, cut into 3 slices, each
- Rapeseed oil: 1 tsp.
- Spinach: 7 oz.
- Softened goat's cheese: 0.8 oz.

Directions

1. Let the oven preheat to 390 F.
2. In a non-stick pan, sauté garlic in a splash of water for a minute.
3. Add spinach and cook until it wilts. Transfer to two small baking dishes with fish on top.
4. Spread cheese on top with tomatoes.
5. Bake for ten minutes. Serve.

Nutrition Per Serving: Kcal 200 | Sodium 44 mg | Protein 26 g | Carbs 3 g | Fat 8 g | Potassium: 301 mg

16. Salmon Protein Bowl

Preparation time: 15 minutes | Cooking time: 10 minutes | Serving: 1

Ingredients

- 1 stalk celery, chopped
- Wild-caught salmon: 4 oz.
- 1/4 leek, sliced
- Broccoli: half head, chopped

- Chopped fresh rosemary, curry powder & chili powder, to taste
- 1/4 avocado, sliced
- Salt & pepper, to taste

Directions

1. Cook salmon as you like.
2. In a pot, add water and salt. Let it boil.
3. Add leeks, celery and broccoli. Broil for ten minutes. Drain all but a half cup of liquid.
4. Pureed the vegetables with a stick blender, add reserved water one tbsp. at a time.
5. Mix in the chili powder, curry, salt, pepper and rosemary.
6. Transfer to a bowl, top with salmon & avocado. Serve.

Nutrition Per Serving: Kcal 374| Sodium 44 mg | Protein 26 g | Carbs 7.7 g | Fat 20.4 g | Potassium: 301 mg

17. Roasted Asian Salmon

Preparation time: 15 minutes| Cooking time: 22 minutes| Serving: 4

Ingredients

- Peanut oil: 2 tsp.
- Asparagus: 1 lb.
- Skinless salmon: 4 fillets
- Salt, to taste
- 1 red bell pepper

For Glaze

- Garlic powder: half tsp.
- Asian sesame oil: 1 tbsp.
- Sweetener: 2 tbsp.
- Unseasoned rice vinegar: 2 tbsp.
- Light soy sauce: 1/3 cup

Directions

1. Let the oven preheat to 400 F. Oil spray a baking sheet.
2. In a bowl, add all the glaze ingredients and mix.
3. Pat dry the salmon and brush with the glaze and let it rest at room temperature.
4. Cut the bell pepper to asparagus size thinly. Spread the asparagus and bell peppers on a baking sheet, toss with oil and salt. Roast for ten minutes.
5. Take the tray out and place fish on one side, brush with glaze again and bake for 10 to 12 minutes.
6. Serve with vegetables with a drizzle of glaze.

Nutrition Per Serving: Kcal 217| Sodium 343 mg | Protein 14 g | Carbs 11.1 g | Fat 10 g | Potassium: 301 mg

18. Salmon with Tomatoes-Olive-Pistachio Tapenade

Preparation time: 15 minutes| Cooking time: 15 minutes| Serving: 4

Ingredients

- Salt & pepper: half tsp., each
- Pistachio nuts: 2 oz., chopped finely
- Green olives: 3 oz., chopped finely
- Salmon: 1½ lbs., boneless fillets
- Olive oil: 2 tbsp.

For tomatoes

- Olive oil: half tbsp.
- Dried thyme: half tbsp.
- Cherry tomatoes: 14 oz.
- Salt & pepper, to taste

Directions

1. Let the oven preheat to 350 F.
2. Toss the pistachios and olives in a bowl with a splash of olive oil, salt and pepper.
3. In a baking dish, add the fish. Spread the pistachio mixture all over the fish.
4. In a different baking dish, add tomatoes, toss with the rest of the ingredients.
5. Bake the tomatoes and fish for 15 minutes. Serve.

Nutrition Per Serving: Kcal 189| Sodium 343 mg | Protein 39 g | Carbs 5 g | Fat 9 g | Potassium: 305 mg

19. Soy & Butter Salmon Parcels

Preparation time: 15 minutes| Cooking time: 15 minutes| Serving: 4

Ingredients

- 4 skinless salmon fillets: 3.5 oz., each
- Light soy sauce: 2 tbsp.
- 2 scallions, sliced
- Honey: 1 tbsp.
- Butter: 2 tbsp.
- Sesame oil: few drops
- Sesame seeds: 1 tbsp.
- 1 cucumber, finely sliced

Directions

1. Place a griddle pan on medium heat.
2. Place each piece of salmon on a foil piece, and oil spray the foil piece.
3. In a bowl, mix honey and soy, pour a little on each piece of salmon and fold to make a packet.
4. Place on the grill pan and cook for 5 to 10 minutes until tender.
5. In a bowl, toss the cucumber with sesame oil and salt. Serve with salmon.

6. Top with sesame seeds

Nutrition Per Serving: Kcal 176| Sodium 301 mg | Protein 19 g | Carbs 2 g | Fat 7.8 g | Potassium: 301 mg

20. Salmon With Cucumber Noodles & Thyme

Preparation time: 15 minutes| Cooking time: 15 minutes| Serving: 2

Ingredients

- 1 fennel bulb, sliced
- 1 large cucumber
- Fresh thyme leaves
- Green olives: half cup, pitted
- 2 wild salmon fillets
- Grass-fed ghee: 3 tbsp.
- Olive oil: 2 tbsp.

Directions

1. Let the oven preheat to 350 F.
2. Oil spray a baking tray with place fennel. Add salmon on top.
3. Add ghee on top with thyme leaves. Bake for 15 minutes.
4. With a spiralizer, noodles the cucumber and squeeze dry. Add to a bowl and toss with olive oil.
5. Serve the salmon with cucumber noodles and olives.

Nutrition Per Serving: Kcal 502| Sodium 773 mg | Protein 39 g | Carbs 16 g | Fat 31 g | Potassium: 897 mg

21. Baked Mayo-Parmesan Fish

Preparation time: 15 minutes| Cooking time: 20 minutes| Serving: 4

Ingredients

- Fish rub: 1 tsp.
- Garlic powder: half tsp.
- Light mayo: half cup
- 4 fish fillets
- Grated parmesan: 4 tbsp., low-fat
- Black pepper, to taste

Directions

1. Pat dry the fish and season with the fish rub.
2. Let the oven preheat to 400 F.
3. In a bowl, add the rest of the ingredients and mix well. Spread the mixture on the fish fillets.
4. Transfer to a baking dish and sprinkle black pepper on top.
5. Bake for 12 minutes. Then, broil for 3 to 4 minutes.
6. Serve.

Nutrition Per Serving: Kcal 637| Sodium 674 mg | Protein 45 g | Carbs 2 g | Fat 26 g | Potassium: 897 mg

22. Baked Parmesan Salmon

Preparation time: 15 minutes| Cooking time: 20 minutes| Serving: 8

Ingredients

- Crushed pork rinds: ¾ cup
- Salt & pepper: 1/8 tsp., each
- Grated parmesan cheese: 2/3 cup, low-fat
- Atlantic salmon: 2 ¼ lbs.
- Minced garlic: 1 tbsp.
- Dried dill: 3 tbsp.
- Melted butter: ¼ cup, unsalted

Directions

1. Let the oven preheat to 450 F. line a baking sheet with foil and oil spray it.
2. In a bowl, add the rest of the ingredients except for fish. Mix well and pour over the fish and coat the fish.
3. Bake the salmon for 15 minutes until the internal temperature reaches 120 F.
4. Broil for 1 to 2 minutes. Serve with fresh parsley on top.

Nutrition Per Serving: Kcal 360| Sodium 248 mg | Protein 36 g | Carbs 1.7 g | Fat 23.4 g | Potassium: 345 mg

23. Seared Salmon With Hollandaise

Preparation time: 15 minutes| Cooking time: 10 minutes| Serving: 4

Ingredients

- Salt & black pepper, to taste
- 1 ¼ lbs. Boneless salmon fillets
- Butter: half tbsp.

Hollandaise
- Salt, to taste
- Melted butter: 7 oz.
- 1 egg
- Lemon juice: 1 tbsp.

Directions

1. In a glass, break the egg and whisk with a stick blender while slowly adding the melted butter, until fluffy.
2. Add lemon juice and salt, mix.
3. Coat the fish in butter, season with salt and pepper.
4. Cook in a pan until fork tender.
5. Serve with sauce.

Nutrition Per Serving: Kcal 307| Sodium 286 mg | Protein 33 g | Carbs 3 g | Fat 6 g | Potassium: 350 mg

24. Coconut Fish Curry

Preparation time: 15 minutes | Cooking time: 15 minutes | Serving: 4

Ingredients

- 1 onion, diced
- 1 minced garlic clove
- Fish pie mix: 13.7 oz.
- Peas: 7 oz.
- Coconut oil: 1 tbsp.
- Turmeric, chili flakes & garam masala: 1 tsp., each
- Canned coconut milk: 13.5 oz.

Directions

1. In a pan, heat oil and sauté onion with a sprinkle of salt for ten minutes.
2. Add spices and garlic cook for 1 minute, with a splash of water.
3. Add milk and cook for ten minutes.
4. Add peas and pie mix cook for 3 minutes. Adjust seasoning and add lime juice.

Serve.

Nutrition Per Serving: Kcal 354 | Sodium 345 mg | Protein 22 g | Carbs 13 g | Fat 23 g | Potassium: 357 mg

25. Dijon Baked Salmon

Preparation time: 15 minutes | Cooking time: 25 minutes | Serving: 5

Ingredients

- Fresh parsley: ¼ cup, chopped
- 3 chopped garlic cloves
- Lemon juice: 1 tbsp.
- 1 1/2 lbs. Of salmon
- Avocado oil: 1 tbsp.
- Dijon mustard: ¼ cup
- Salt & pepper, to taste

Directions

- Let the oven preheat to 375 F.
- Add all ingredients except for fish in a bowl and mix. Spread all over the salmon and coat well.
- Bake for 18 to 20 minutes. Slice & serve.

Nutrition Per Serving: Kcal 249 | Sodium 371 mg | Protein 30.5 g | Carbs 1.9 g | Fat 13.4 g | Potassium: 327 mg

26. Salmon Patties With Sauce

Preparation time: 30 minutes | Cooking time: 10 minutes | Serving: 6

Ingredients

- Almond flour: 3 tbsp.
- Capers: 1 tbsp., drained & chopped
- Hemp seeds: 3 tbsp.
- 2 cans of (6oz.) Salmon, drained
- 2 eggs
- Green onion: 3 tbsp., chopped
- Fish rub: 1 tsp.
- Olive oil: 2 tbsp.
- Salt and pepper, to taste

Directions

1. Shred the drained salmon apart. Mix with the rest of the ingredients except for eggs & oil.
2. Whisk eggs and add to the bowl, and mix gently.
3. Make into 6 patties and place on a baking sheet. Keep in the freezer for 15 minutes.
4. In a pan, heat oil and cook the patties for 3 to 4 minutes on each side.
5. Serve with sauce.

Nutrition Per Serving: Kcal 232 | Sodium 190 mg | Protein 17 g | Carbs 2 g | Fat 17 g | Potassium: 309 mg

27. Seared Scallops & Cauliflower Rice Risotto

Preparation time: 15 minutes | Cooking time: 25 minutes | Serving: 4

Ingredients

- Salt & pepper, to taste
- Jumbo scallops: 1 lb.
- Olive oil: 2 tbsp.

Cauliflower risotto

- Green onions: ¼ cup, sliced
- 3 minced garlic cloves
- Salt & pepper: ¼ tsp., each
- Butter: 3 tbsp.
- Low-fat cream: 1 cup
- Riced cauliflower: 4 cups
- Broccoli florets: 1 cup, chopped
- Low-fat parmesan Cheese: 3/4 cup

Directions

1. Place a skillet on medium flame. Add butter, scallions and broccoli. Cook for 3 minutes.
2. Add riced cauliflower and cook for 3 minutes.
3. Add the rest of the ingredients and mix cheese. Simmer on low flame until tender. Set it aside.

4. Pat dry the scallops and season with salt and pepper. In a pan, add oil and let it get hot.
5. Add scallops and cook for 2 minutes on each side. Turn the heat off.
6. Serve with risotto and green onions on top.

Nutrition Per Serving: Kcal 551 | Sodium 768 mg | Protein 23 g | Carbs 12 g | Fat 47 g | Potassium: 686 mg

28. Seafood Chowder

Preparation time: 15 minutes | Cooking time: 20 minutes | Serving: 4

Ingredients

- 2 minced garlic cloves
- Half lemon's juice & zest
- Celery stalks: 1 ½ cups, sliced
- Shrimp: 8 oz., peeled & deveined
- Olive oil: 4 tbsp.
- Clam juice: 1 cup
- Low-fat cream cheese: 4 oz.
- Red chili flakes: half tbsp.
- Low-fat cream: 1 ½ cups
- Boneless 1" pieces of salmon: 1 lb.
- Dried thyme: 2 tsp.
- Baby spinach: 2 oz.
- Salt & black pepper, to taste

Directions

1. In a pot, heat the olive oil and saute garlic, celery for 5 minutes.
2. Add zest, juice, thyme, cream cheese, cream and clam juice. Simmer for ten minutes.
3. Add shrimps and fish, cook for 3 minutes.
4. Add salt and pepper. Add the rest of the ingredients on top, serve.

Nutrition Per Serving: Kcal 402 | Sodium 382 mg | Protein 37 g | Carbs 6 g | Fat 8 g | Potassium: 601 mg

29. Cashew, Chilli & Lime-Crusted Fish

Preparation time: 15 minutes | Cooking time: 15 minutes | Serving: 4

Ingredients

- Lime juice: 5 tbsp.
- 1 grated garlic clove
- Vegetable oil: 1 tbsp.
- 4 skinless white fish fillets

For crust
- 4 mild red chilies
- Cumin powder: 1 tbsp.
- Vegetable oil: 2 tbsp.
- Cashews: 3.5 oz.
- 6 peeled garlic cloves
- 1-inch piece of ginger, chopped

Directions

1. In a bowl, add oil, garlic and lime juice (2 tbsp.) mix.
2. Rub all over the fish and let it rest for 20 to 30 minutes.
3. Let the oven preheat to 375 F.
4. In a bowl, add all the crust's ingredients with the rest of the lime juice. Spread on the fish.
5. Bake for 12 to 15 minutes, serve.

Nutrition Per Serving: Kcal 356 | Sodium 371 mg | Protein 32 g | Carbs 8 g | Fat 22 g | Potassium: 551 mg

30. Tandoori Salmon

Preparation time: 20 minutes | Cooking time: 10 minutes | Serving: 2

Ingredients

- Low-fat yogurt: 6 oz.
- Green cardamom seeds: 1 tsp.
- Turmeric: 1 tsp.
- Apple cider: 1 tbsp.
- Cumin seeds: 1 tsp.
- Cloves: 1 tsp.
- Avocado oil: 1 tbsp.
- Ground ginger: 1 tsp.
- 2 salmon fillets: 4 oz., each
- Cinnamon: 1 tsp.

Directions

1. In a bowl, add all spices and yogurt mix and spread all over the salmon.
2. Let it rest for half an hour.
3. Let the oven preheat to 350 F. Place the salmon on a foil-lined baking sheet.
4. Bake for 5 minutes, broil for 2 to 3 minutes.
5. Serve with cauliflower rice.

Nutrition Per Serving: Kcal 432 | Sodium 389 mg | Protein 34 g | Carbs 13.9 g | Fat 23 g | Potassium: 401 mg

31. Asian Shrimp & Brussels Sprouts

Preparation time: 15 minutes | Cooking time: 23 minutes | Serving: 4

Ingredients

- Salt and pepper, to taste
- Brussels sprouts: 1 lb., halved & trimmed
- Jumbo shrimp: 1 lb.
- Olive oil: 2 tbsp.

For sauce
- Rice vinegar: 2 tbsp.
- Garlic powder: half tsp.
- Granulated sweetener: 2 tbsp.
- Light soy sauce: 1/3 cup

- Agave nectar: 2 tsp.
- Sesame oil: 1 tbsp.

Directions

1. Pat dry the shrimps.
2. In a bowl, add all ingredients of sauce and mix.
3. Let the oven preheat to 400 F. oil spray a baking sheet.
4. In a ziplock bag, add dried shrimps and sauce (half) and shake well. Let them rest.
5. Toss the Brussels with oil, salt and pepper and spread on a baking sheet. Roast for 15 minutes.
6. Take the shrimps out of the marinade and place with the sprouts in one even layer.
7. Roast for 6 to 8 minutes. Serve with a drizzle of sauce.

Nutrition Per Serving: Kcal 296| Sodium 544 mg | Protein 31 g | Carbs 9 g | Fat 13 g | Potassium: 561 mg

32. Brazilian Fish Stew

Preparation time: 15 minutes| Cooking time: 40 minutes| Serving: 5

Ingredients

For Base

- 1 sliced red bell pepper
- Canned crushed tomatoes: 14 oz.
- 1 onion, chopped
- Smoked paprika: 1 tbsp.
- Fish broth: 1 cup
- Canned coconut milk: ¾ cup
- Coconut oil: 2 tbsp.
- 5 grated cloves of garlic
- Cayenne: ¼ tsp.
- Black pepper: half tsp.
- Ground cumin: 1 tbsp.
- Table salt: 1 tsp.

For finishing

- Chopped parsley: 1 tbsp.
- White fish: 1 ½ pound
- Coconut oil: 2 tbsp.
- Lime juice: 1 tbsp.

Directions

1. In a pressure cooker, add all ingredients of the base, stir. Cook, sealed for ten minutes on high pressure.
2. Pat dry the fish and remove any bones & skin. Slice into 1" pieces.
3. Release the pressure and select the saute mode. Let it come to a boil, simmer for ten minutes.
4. Add fish and cook for 5 minutes.
5. Add the rest of the ingredients, cook for few minutes, serve.

Nutrition Per Serving: Kcal 330| Sodium 690 mg | Protein 28 g | Carbs 9 g | Fat 18 g | Potassium: 561 mg

33. Scrambled Eggs With Smoked Salmon

Preparation time: 15 minutes| Cooking time: 10 minutes| Serving: 2

Ingredients

- Cream: 2 tbsp., low-fat
- Smoked salmon: 2 oz.
- Baby spinach: 1 oz.
- 2 eggs
- Salt and black pepper, to taste
- Butter: 1 tbsp.

Directions

1. Saute spinach in butter for few minutes.
2. Add cream and cook for few minutes.
3. Add eggs and mix well. Sprinkle salt and pepper, cooking to scramble.
4. Serve with smoked salmon on top.

Nutrition Per Serving: Kcal 201| Sodium 390 mg | Protein 13 g | Carbs 4.5 g | Fat 12 g | Potassium: 406 mg

34. Crisp-Skin Fish

Preparation time: 15 minutes| Cooking time: 10 minutes| Serving: 4

Ingredients

- 24 asparagus spears, trimmed
- 2 tomatoes, diced without seeds
- Olive oil: 1 tbsp.
- 4 salmon fillets

Dressing

- Parsley leaves: 2 tbsp., chopped
- Black olives: 1 tbsp.
- Olive oil: 3 tbsp.
- Capers: 1 tbsp., rinsed

Directions

1. In a pan, heat oil.
2. Season the fish with salt and pepper. Place in the pan skin side down, cook for 3 to 4 minutes.
3. Flip and cook for 3 to 4 minutes. Take it out on a plate.
4. Boil the asparagus for 3 to 4 minutes, drain.
5. In the pan, heat some oil and sauté dressing ingredients, add asparagus and toss.
6. Serve with the fish.

Nutrition Per Serving: Kcal 297| Sodium 390 mg | Protein 35 g | Carbs 3 g | Fat 16 g | Potassium: 406 mg

35. Wild Baked Salmon

Preparation time: 15 minutes | Cooking time: 10 minutes | Serving: 4

Ingredients

- 2 cups of asparagus
- Lemon juice: 1 tbsp.
- Sliced fennel: half cup
- Dried kelp: 1 tbsp.
- 2 avocados
- Wild salmon: 21 oz.
- Olive oil: 1 tbsp.
- Coconut aminos: 1 tbsp.
- Himalayan pink salt: 1 tsp.

Directions

1. In a bowl, add lemon juice, salt, coconut aminos, and kelp. Mix and add fish coat well.
2. Let it rest for 20 minutes.
3. Let the oven preheat to 350 F. Steam the asparagus.
4. In a pan, add fennel place fish on top. Bake for 10 minutes.
5. Serve the fish with asparagus and fennel. Drizzle with olive oil and sprinkle with salt, serve.

Nutrition Per Serving: Kcal 538 | Sodium 450 mg | Protein 46 g | Carbs 10 g | Fat 33 g | Potassium: 612 mg

36. Green Beans & Shrimp Sheet Pan Meal

Preparation time: 15 minutes | Cooking time: 18 minutes | Serving: 4

Ingredients

- 2 lemons' zest
- Salt & pepper: 1 tsp., each
- Olive oil: 4 tbsp.
- Aleppo pepper: 1/8 tsp.
- Extra-large raw shrimp: 1 lb.
- Green beans: 1 lb., trimmed
- Ground cumin & ground coriander: half tsp., each

Directions

1. Let the oven preheat to 425 F.
2. In a bowl, add shrimps with lemon zest, half of the olive oil, salt and pepper. Toss and let it rest.
3. Cut the beans into small pieces, toss with the rest of the salt, pepper, oil and the rest of the ingredients.
4. Roast for ten minutes on a baking sheet, stirring as needed.
5. Take the tray out, add shrimps, roast for 6 to 8 minutes.
6. Serve with a drizzle of lemon juice.

Nutrition Per Serving: Kcal 243 | Sodium 778 mg | Protein 18 g | Carbs 11 g | Fat 15 g | Potassium: 712 mg

37. Fish Taco Bowls

Preparation time: 15 minutes | Cooking time: 10 minutes | Serving: 4

Ingredients

- 4 filets Tilpia
- 4 Limes
- Garlic Powder & cayenne: ¼ tsp., each
- Avocado Oil: 1 tbsp.
- Green Cabbage: 2 cups, shredded
- Salt, to taste
- Cumin & chili powder: half tsp., each
- Lite Mayo: half cup
- Cilantro: 2 tbsp. chopped

Directions

1. In a bowl, toss the cabbage with half tsp. of salt and one lime juice.
2. In a different bowl, add cilantro, mayo and one lime juice. Mix.
3. Add the rest of the ingredients (except for oil) to a bowl, and season the fish with it.
4. In a pan, add oil and cook fish for 3 to 4 minutes on 1 side.
5. In each serving bowl, add cabbage, then fish, top with sauce and serve.

Nutrition Per Serving: Kcal 256 | Sodium 767 mg | Protein 2 g | Carbs 10 g | Fat 25 g | Potassium: 166 mg

38. Creamy Fish Casserole

Preparation time: 15 minutes | Cooking time: 30 minutes | Serving: 4

Ingredients

- Small florets broccoli: 1 lb.
- Salt: 1 tsp.
- Small capers: 2 tbsp.
- Dijon mustard: 1 tbsp.
- Black pepper: half tsp.
- Olive oil: 3 tbsp.
- Dried parsley: 1 tbsp.
- Scallions: 1 ¼ cups, chopped
- Low-fat cream: 1 ¼ cups
- White fish: 1 ½ lbs., cut into fillets

Directions

1. Let the oven preheat to 400 F. oil spray a 13 by 9" baking dish.

2. In a pan, heat oil and sauté broccoli for 5 minutes, sprinkle with salt and pepper.
3. Add capers, scallions and cook for few minutes. Transfer to the baking dish.
4. Add fish on top.
5. Add the rest of the ingredients to a bowl, mix and pour over salmon.
6. Bake for 20 minutes, serve.

Nutrition Per Serving: Kcal 456 | Sodium 767 mg | Protein 39 g | Carbs 8 g | Fat 12 g | Potassium: 319 mg

39. Ginger & Soy Salmon

Preparation time: 15 minutes | Cooking time: 25 minutes | Serving: 2

Ingredients

- Rice wine vinegar: 1 tbsp.
- 1 red chili, sliced with seeds
- 1" piece of ginger, grated
- 1 carrot, spiralized into noodles
- 1 grated garlic clove
- Light soy sauce: 2 tbsp.
- 2 salmon fillets, skinless
- 1 courgette, spiralized into noodles
- Bok choi: 2 bulbs, separated leaves

Directions

1. Let the oven preheat to 350 F.
2. In a bowl, mix ginger, vinegar, soy, garlic and black pepper. Add fish and coat well; let it rest for ten minutes.
3. Take 2 parchment paper sheets and divide the vegetables; add salmon on top with marinade. Fold to seal the packet.
4. Bake for 20 to 25 minutes. Serve

Nutrition Per Serving: Kcal 391 | Sodium 367 mg | Protein 39 g | Carbs 9 g | Fat 12 g | Potassium: 319 mg

40. Halibut Ceviche

Preparation time: 15 minutes | Cooking time: 10 minutes | Serving: 2

Ingredients

- 1 lime's juice
- wild-caught halibut: 8 oz., cubed
- Himalayan pink salt, a pinch
- fresh cilantro: 2 tbsp., chopped
- Olive Oil: 2 tsp.
- 1 avocado, cubed
- 1 green onion, sliced

Directions

1. Add oil, juice and salt to a bowl and mix. Add the rest of the ingredients and toss to coat.
2. Let it rest few hours in the fridge. Serve.

Nutrition Per Serving: Kcal 198 | Sodium 367 mg | Protein 20 g | Carbs 2 g | Fat 12 g | Potassium: 319 mg

41. Baked Salmon With Pesto & Tomatoes

Preparation time: 15 minutes | Cooking time: 15 minutes | Serving: 2

Ingredients

- 2 tomatoes, cut into ¼" thick
- Fish rub, as needed
- 2 salmon fillets: 6 oz., each
- Basil pesto: 4 tsp.

Directions

1. Let the oven preheat to 450 F, with a baking sheet.
2. Place each piece of salmon in a big foil piece, oil spray the foil sheets.
3. Season the fish with the fish rub. Add pesto on top and spread.
4. Place tomato slices on pesto, wrap in foil and seal the edges.
5. Place on the heated sheet and bake for 15 minutes, let it rest for 2 to 3 minutes, then serve.

Nutrition Per Serving: Kcal 575 | Sodium 211 mg | Protein 62 g | Carbs 6 g | Fat 33 g | Potassium: 319 mg

42. Tzatziki Avocado Salmon Rolls

Preparation time: 30 minutes | Cooking time: 0 minutes | Serving: 4

Ingredients

- Minced chives: 2 tbsp.
- 1/4 lime's juice
- 8 seedless cucumber strips & 12 rounds
- Thick tzatziki: 2 tbsp.
- Mix sesame seeds: 2 tbsp.
- Half avocado
- Wild smoked salmon: 5 oz.

Directions

1. In a bowl, add tzatziki, lime juice and chives (1 tsp.)
2. Place a 16" long plastic wrap on a table and overlap salmon pieces to make a 12 by 7" rectangle. Press down lightly.
3. Add tzatziki mixture on top and spread. Add avocado slices on top, then cucumber strips and the rest of the chives.
4. With the plastic, roll the salmon and sprinkle seeds on top. Keep the roll in the fridge for 15 minutes, slice and place on cucumber rounds.

5. Serve.

Nutrition Per Serving: Kcal 139| Sodium 765 mg | Protein 9.5 g | Carbs 6 g | Fat 8.4 g | Potassium: 469 mg

43. Thai Fish Curry

Preparation time: 10 minutes | Cooking time: 20 minutes | Serving: 4

Ingredients

- Coconut oil: 1 oz.
- Fresh cilantro: half cup, chopped
- Cauliflower: 1 lb.
- Red or green curry paste: 2 tbsp.
- Salt & pepper, to taste
- Boneless salmon fillets: 1½ lbs., in pieces
- Coconut cream: 2 cups

Directions

1. Let the oven preheat to 400 F. Oil spray a medium baking dish.
2. Add fish to the dish and season with salt and pepper, drizzle with oil.
3. In a bowl, add cilantro, coconut cream, and curry paste mix, pour on the fish, stir, and bake for 20 minutes.
4. Boil or steam the florets and serve with the curry.

Nutrition Per Serving: Kcal 333| Sodium 345 mg | Protein 42 g | Carbs 3.4 g | Fat 8 g | Potassium: 309 mg

44. Roast Salmon With Preserved Lemon

Preparation time: 3 hours | Cooking time: 25 minutes | Serving: 4

Ingredients

- Broth: 3.3 oz.
- Wild salmon: 35 oz.
- Sea salt, to taste
- Preserved lemon: 1.4 oz., without flesh & pith
- Dill: a half bunch
- Chilli flakes: 1 tsp.
- Granulated sugar substitute: 1.7 oz.
- Thyme leaves: 1 tsp.

Roasting oil

- Olive oil: 4 tbsp.
- Preserved lemons: 1 oz., without seeds

Directions

1. Add broth and preserved lemon to a food processor. Pulse until smooth.
2. In a pan, place fish and spread this mixture on top.
3. In a bowl, add thyme, salt, chili flakes and sugar substitute. Mix and sprinkle over the fish and cover with plastic wrap.
4. Keep in the fridge for 2 hours.
5. Let the oven preheat to 320 F. Let the fish rest at room temperature for half an hour before cooking.
6. In a food processor, add the roasting oil's ingredients and pulse until smooth.
7. Take the fish out and pat dry. Place on a baking sheet and drizzle with roasting oil; coat the fish.
8. Wrap in foil and bake for 15 minutes. Take the foil off, bake for ten minutes more.
9. Serve with dill on top.

Nutrition Per Serving: Kcal 397| Sodium 345 mg | Protein 35 g | Carbs 1 g | Fat 21 g | Potassium: 267 mg

45. Fish Cakes With Lemon Avocado Sauce

Preparation time: 15 minutes | Cooking time: 10 minutes | Serving: 6

Ingredients

- Fresh cilantro: ¼ cup, chopped
- Coconut oil: 1 to 2 tbsp.
- Boneless white fish: 1 pound
- Salt & chili flakes, a pinch
- 1 to 2 garlic cloves

Dipping sauce

- 1 lemon's juice
- Water: 2 tbsp.
- Salt, a pinch
- 2 avocados

Directions

1. Add all ingredients except for oil to a food processor, pulse until combined.
2. In a pan, add oil and heat. Make the mixture into 6 patties.
3. Place in hot oil, cook for a few minutes on both sides until cooked.
4. In a food processor, add all ingredients of the sauce. Pulse until smooth, adjust seasoning and serve with fish cakes.

Nutrition Per Serving: Kcal 69| Sodium 215 mg | Protein 1.1 g | Carbs 2.7 g | Fat 6.5 g | Potassium: 227 mg

46. Baked Halibut

Preparation time: 15 minutes | Cooking time: 24 minutes | Serving: 2

Ingredients

- Garlic powder & dill weed: ¼ tsp., each
- Salt & pepper, to taste
- Sliced scallions: 2 tbsp.
- 2 fillets of halibut
- Sour cream: 3 tbsp.

- Low-fat parmesan cheese: 2 tbsp., grated

Directions

1. Pat dry the fish. Let the oven preheat to 375 F.
2. In a bowl, add all ingredients except for fish. Mix well. Spread all over the fish.
3. Bake for 24 minutes until the internal temperature reaches 145 F.
4. Serve.

Nutrition Per Serving: Kcal 290| Sodium 508 mg | Protein 40 g | Carbs 3 g | Fat 12 g | Potassium: 276 mg

47. Roasted Spiced Cod With Brussels Sprouts

Preparation time: 15 minutes| Cooking time: 24 minutes| Serving: 4

Ingredients

- 2 garlic cloves, grated
- Lemon juice: 2 to 3 tbsp.
- Ground paprika: 1 tsp.
- Brussels sprouts: half lb., halved
- Onion powder: 1 tsp.
- Ground cumin: 1 tsp.
- Olive oil: 2 tbsp.
- Sea salt: half tsp.
- Ground coriander: 1 tsp.
- Olive oil: 3 tbsp.
- 10 cherry tomatoes
- 4 cod fillets
- Half lemon's zest
- Half red chili, chopped
- Salt: half tsp.

Directions

1. Let the oven preheat to 400 F
2. Add all ingredients to a bowl except for fish, tomato and Brussels sprouts.
3. Oil spray a parchment-lined baking sheet, place fish on top, top with spice mixture, and place Brussels sprouts around the fish. Top the fish with tomato slices.
4. Drizzle with some olive oil, sprinkle sea salt.
5. Bake for 20 minutes on the middle shelf. Serve.

Nutrition Per Serving: Kcal 199| Sodium 217 mg | Protein 13 g | Carbs 2 g | Fat 5 g | Potassium: 221 mg

48. Foil Baked Chilean Sea Bass

Preparation time: 15 minutes| Cooking time: 15 minutes| Serving: 2

Ingredients

- Fresh Leaf Spinach: 12 oz.
- Black Pepper, sea salt & creole seasoning: 1 tsp., each
- Low-fat Whipping Cream: ¼ cup
- Butter: 2 tbsp.
- Chilean Sea Bass: 1 lb.
- Minced Garlic: 2 tsp.

Directions

1. Let the oven preheat to 400 F.
2. Season the fish with Black Pepper, sea salt & creole seasoning.
3. In a pan, add butter on medium flame. Saute garlic for 1 minute, add spinach and cream.
4. Cook until it wilts slightly, turns the heat off.
5. Divide spinach in 2 foil sheets. Place fish on top and seal the foil into a packet.
6. Bake for 12 minutes.

Nutrition Per Serving: Kcal 415| Sodium 298 mg | Protein 14.5 g | Carbs 3 g | Fat 15 g | Potassium: 280 mg

49. Grilled Salmon With Avocado Topping

Preparation time: 15 minutes| Cooking time: 15 minutes| Serving: 4

Ingredients

For Fish

- Avocado oil: 2 tbsp.
- Boneless salmon fillets: 1½ lbs.
- Coarse salt: 1 tsp.
- Black pepper: half tsp.

Avocado topping

- Half red onion, chopped
- Olive oil: 1 tbsp.
- Cherry tomatoes: 1¼ cups, quartered
- 2 avocados, diced
- Lime juice: 2 tbsp.
- Black pepper: half tsp.
- Salt: 1 tsp.

Directions

1. Oil spray the grill grates and heat to medium-low or till 300 F.
2. Coat the fish in olive oil and season with salt and pepper.
3. Grill the salmon for 10 to 15 minutes or to your desired consistency.

4. In a bowl, add all ingredients of avocado topping, toss and serve on top of the grilled fish.

Nutrition Per Serving: Kcal 620 | Sodium 298 mg | Protein 37 g | Carbs 5 g | Fat 13 g | Potassium: 309 mg

50. Garlic & Lemon Shrimp

Preparation time: 10 minutes | Cooking time: 7 minutes | Serving: 4

Ingredients

- Olive oil: 2 tbsp.
- Lemon juice: 2 tbsp.
- Jumbo shrimp: 1 lb.
- Butter: 1 tbsp.
- Sea salt, to taste
- Minced garlic: 2 tbsp.
- Lemon zest: 1 tbsp.

Directions

1. Pat dry the shrimp.
2. In a pan, add oil and butter on medium flame. Add shrimp and cook for 1 to 2 minutes.
3. Add garlic and cook for 3 to 4 minutes. Turn off the heat and add the rest of the ingredients, toss well and serve.

Nutrition Per Serving: Kcal 229 | Sodium 765 mg | Protein 26 g | Carbs 4 g | Fat 12 g | Potassium: 319 mg

51. Easy Roasted Salmon

Preparation time: 15 minutes | Cooking time: 25 minutes | Serving: 4

Ingredients

- Fresh dill: ¼ cup, chopped
- 4 garlic cloves, minced
- One lemon, cut into fours
- Black pepper, to taste
- 4 salmon fillets

Directions

1. Preheat the oven to 400 F.
2. Place the fish in an oil spryed baking dish, drizzle with lemon juice.
3. Season with the rest of the ingredients.
4. Bake for 20 to 22 minutes. Serve.

Nutrition Per Serving: Kcal 251 | Sodium 78 mg | Protein 34 g | Carbs 3 g | Fat 2 g | Potassium: 209 mg

52. Garlic Lemon Shrimp

Preparation time: 15 minutes | Cooking time: 8 minutes | Serving: 4

Ingredients

- Lemon juice: 1 tbsp.
- Ground cumin: 1 tsp.
- Olive oil: 2 tbsp.
- 3 garlic cloves, sliced
- 1 pound Shrimp, peeled & deveined
- Fresh parsley: 2 tbsp., chopped
- Salt: ¼ tsp.

Directions

1. Cook shrimp for 3 minutes in oil, add all the ingredients.
2. Cook for 2-3 minutes.
3. Serve.

Nutrition Per Serving: Kcal 163 | Sodium 284 mg | Protein 19 g | Carbs 2 g | Fat 8 g | Potassium: 187 mg

53. Scallops with Snow Peas & Orange

Preparation time: 15 minutes | Cooking time: 12 minutes | Serving: 4

Ingredients

- 1 orange
- Black pepper, to taste
- Snow peas: 3/4 pound, halved lengthwise
- 16 sea scallops
- Olive oil: 1 tbsp. & 2 tsp.
- Dry Couscous: 1 cup, cooked

Directions

1. Season the scallops with salt and pepper.
2. Cook in hot oil for 2 to 3 minutes on side, take them out.
3. Thinly slice an orange peel (only 1/8th part).
4. Sauté snow peas with orange peel, with salt and pepper.
5. Serve with scallops and couscous

Nutrition Per Serving: Kcal 298 | Sodium 123 mg | Protein 19 g | Carbs 2 g | Fat 11 g | Potassium: 187 mg

Chapter 8: 8-Week Meal Plan

COOKING CONVERSION CHART

Measurement

CUP	ONCES	MILLILITERS	TABLESPOONS
8 cup	64 oz	1895 ml	128
6 cup	48 oz	1420 ml	96
5 cup	40 oz	1180 ml	80
4 cup	32 oz	960 ml	64
2 cup	16 oz	480 ml	32
1 cup	8 oz	240 ml	16
3/4 cup	6 oz	177 ml	12
2/3 cup	5 oz	158 ml	11
1/2 cup	4 oz	118 ml	8
3/8 cup	3 oz	90 ml	6
1/3 cup	2.5 oz	79 ml	5.5
1/4 cup	2 oz	59 ml	4
1/8 cup	1 oz	30 ml	3
1/16 cup	1/2 oz	15 ml	1

Temperature

FAHRENHEIT	CELSIUS
100 °F	37 °C
150 °F	65 °C
200 °F	93 °C
250 °F	121 °C
300 °F	150 °C
325 °F	160 °C
350 °F	180 °C
375 °F	190 °C
400 °F	200 °C
425 °F	220 °C
450 °F	230 °C
500 °F	260 °C
525 °F	274 °C
550 °F	288 °C

Weight

IMPERIAL	METRIC
1/2 oz	15 g
1 oz	29 g
2 oz	57 g
3 oz	85 g
4 oz	113 g
5 oz	141 g
6 oz	170 g
8 oz	227 g
10 oz	283 g
12 oz	340 g
13 oz	369 g
14 oz	397 g
15 oz	425 g
1 lb	453 g

Stage-1: Week 1

Use protein powder in the milk to get your daily recommended dose of protein if advised by your doctor or dietitian. Do not forget to drink water. You also can drink decaffeinated coffee or tea.

- **Monday**
    - Breakfast: 3.5 oz. of semi-skimmed lactose-free milk
    - Snack: 3.5 oz. of low-fat
    - Lunch: 3.5 oz. of Fat-Free Chicken Broth
    - Snack: 1-2 oz. of semi-skimmed lactose-free milk
    - Dinner: 3.5 oz. of Low-Fat Vegetable Broth

- **Tuesday**
  - Breakfast: 3.5 oz. of semi-skimmed lactose-free milk
  - Snack: 3.5 oz. of low-fat
  - Lunch: 3.5 oz. of Fat-Free Chicken Broth
  - Snack: 1-2 oz. of semi-skimmed lactose-free milk
  - Dinner: 3.5 oz. of Low-Fat Vegetable Broth
- **Wednesday**
  - Breakfast: 3.5 oz. of semi-skimmed lactose-free milk
  - Snack: 3.5 oz. of low-fat
  - Lunch: 3.5 oz. of Fat-Free Beef Bone Broth
  - Snack: 1-2 oz. of semi-skimmed lactose-free milk
  - Dinner: 3.5 oz. of Low-Fat Vegetable Broth
- **Thursday**
  - Breakfast: 3.5 oz. of semi-skimmed lactose-free milk
  - Snack: 3.5 oz. of low-fat
  - Lunch: 3.5 oz. of Fat-Free Chicken Broth
  - Snack: 1-2 oz. of semi-skimmed lactose-free milk
  - Dinner: 3.5 oz. of Low-Fat Beef Bone Broth
- **Friday**
  - Breakfast: 3.5 oz. of semi-skimmed lactose-free milk
  - Snack: 3.5 oz. of sugar-free jello
  - Lunch: 3.5 oz. of Fat-Free Chicken Broth
  - Snack: 1-2 oz. of semi-skimmed lactose-free milk
  - Dinner: 3.5 oz. of Low-Fat Vegetable Broth
- **Saturday**
  - Breakfast: 3.5 oz. of semi-skimmed lactose-free milk
  - Snack: 3.5 oz. of low-fat, sugar-free jello
  - Lunch: 3.5 oz. of Fat-Free Beef Bone Broth
  - Snack: 1-2 oz. of sugar-free jello
  - Dinner: 3.5 oz. of Low-Fat Vegetable Broth
- **Sunday**
  - Breakfast: 3.5 oz. of semi-skimmed lactose free milk
  - Snack: 3.5 oz. of low-fat jello

- Lunch: 3.5 oz. of Fat-Free Chicken Broth
- Snack: 1-2 oz. of semi-skimmed lactose-free milk
- Dinner: 3.5 oz. of Low-Fat Vegetable Broth

Week 2

- **Monday**
    - Breakfast: 3.5 oz. of semi-skimmed lactose-free milk
    - Snack: 3.5 oz. of low-fat jello
    - Lunch: 3.5 oz. of Fat-Free Chicken Broth
    - Snack: 1-2 oz. of semi-skimmed lactose-free milk
    - Dinner: 3.5 oz. of Low-Fat Vegetable Broth
- **Tuesday**
    - Breakfast: 3.5 oz. of semi-skimmed lactose-free milk
    - Snack: 3.5 oz. of low-fat jello
    - Lunch: 3.5 oz. of Fat-Free Chicken Broth
    - Snack: 1-2 oz. of semi-skimmed lactose-free milk
    - Dinner: 3.5 oz. of Low-Fat beef bone broth
- **Wednesday**
    - Breakfast: 3.5 oz. of semi-skimmed lactose-free milk
    - Snack: 3.5 oz. of low-fat diluted fruit fresh juice
    - Lunch: 3.5 oz. of Fat-Free Chicken Broth
    - Snack: 1-2 oz. of semi-skimmed lactose-free milk
    - Dinner: 3.5 oz. of Low-Fat Vegetable Broth
- **Thursday**
    - Breakfast: 3.5 oz. of semi-skimmed lactose-free milk
    - Snack: 3.5 oz. of diluted fruit fresh juice
    - Lunch: 3.5 oz. of Fat-Free Chicken Broth
    - Snack: 1-2 oz. of semi-skimmed lactose-free milk
    - Dinner: 3.5 oz. of Low-Fat Beef bone broth
- **Friday**
    - Breakfast: 3.5 oz. of semi-skimmed lactose-free milk
    - Snack: 3.5 oz. of low-fat diluted fruit fresh juice

- Lunch: 3.5 oz. of Fat-Free Chicken Broth
- Snack: 1-2 oz. of semi-skimmed lactose-free milk
- Dinner: 3.5 oz. of Low-Fat Beef bone broth

- **Saturday**
    - Breakfast: 3.5 oz. of semi-skimmed lactose-free milk
    - Snack: 3.5 oz. of low-fat diluted fruit fresh juice
    - Lunch: 3.5 oz. of Fat-Free beef bone broth
    - Snack: 1-2 oz. of semi-skimmed lactose-free milk
    - Dinner: 3.5 oz. of Low-Fat Vegetable Broth
- **Sunday**
    - Breakfast: 3.5 oz. of semi-skimmed lactose-free milk
    - Snack: 3.5 oz. of low-fat diluted fruit fresh juice
    - Lunch: 3.5 oz. of Fat-Free Beef bone broth
    - Snack: 1-2 oz. of semi-skimmed lactose-free milk
    - Dinner: 3.5 oz. of Low-Fat Vegetable Broth

Week 3

- **Monday**
    - Breakfast: 3.5 oz. of semi-skimmed lactose-free milk
    - Snack: 3.5 oz. of low-fat beef bone broth
    - Lunch: 3.5 oz. of Fat-Free Chicken Broth
    - Snack: 1-2 oz. of semi-skimmed lactose-free milk
    - Dinner: 3.5 oz. of Low-Fat Vegetable Broth
- **Tuesday**
    - Breakfast: 3.5 oz. of semi-skimmed lactose-free milk
    - Snack: 3.5 oz. of low-fat diluted fruit fresh juice
    - Lunch: 3.5 oz. of Fat-Free Chicken Broth
    - Snack: 1-2 oz. of semi-skimmed lactose-free milk
    - Dinner: 3.5 oz. of Low-Fat Vegetable Broth
- **Wednesday**
    - Breakfast: 3.5 oz. of semi-skimmed lactose-free milk
    - Snack: 3.5 oz. of low-fat beef bone broth

- Lunch: 3.5 oz. of Fat-Free Chicken Broth
- Snack: 1-2 oz. of semi-skimmed lactose-free milk
- Dinner: 3.5 oz. of Low-Fat Vegetable Broth

- **Thursday**
  - Breakfast: 3.5 oz. of semi-skimmed lactose-free milk
  - Snack: 3.5 oz. of low-fat, sugar-free jello
  - Lunch: 3.5 oz. of Fat-Free Chicken Broth
  - Snack: 1-2 oz. of semi-skimmed lactose-free milk
  - Dinner: 3.5 oz. of Low-Fat Vegetable Broth
- **Friday**
  - Breakfast: 3.5 oz. of semi-skimmed lactose-free milk
  - Snack: 3.5 oz. of low-fat diluted fruit fresh juice
  - Lunch: 3.5 oz. of Fat-Free beef bone broth
  - Snack: 1-2 oz. of semi-skimmed lactose-free milk
  - Dinner: 3.5 oz. of Low-Fat Vegetable Broth
- **Saturday**
  - Breakfast: 3.5 oz. of semi-skimmed lactose-free milk
  - Snack: 3.5 oz. of low-fat jello
  - Lunch: 3.5 oz. of Fat-Free Chicken Broth
  - Snack: 1-2 oz. of semi-skimmed lactose-free milk
  - Dinner: 3.5 oz. of Low-Fat beef bone broth
- **Sunday**
  - Breakfast: 3.5 oz. of semi-skimmed lactose-free milk
  - Snack: 3.5 oz. of low-fat diluted fruit fresh juice
  - Lunch: 3.5 oz. of Fat-Free Chicken Broth
  - Snack: 1-2 oz. of semi-skimmed lactose-free milk
  - Dinner: 3.5 oz. of Low-Fat Vegetable Broth

Stage 2: Week 4

You can follow the provided quantities (in the first week) for the rest of the meals in stage 2 or follow your dietitian's or doctor's advice. Do not forget to take your vitamins & supplements if given by the doctor. Always listen to your body; that is okay too if you feel fuller before finishing your meal.

- **Monday**
    - Breakfast: 3.5 oz. of skim lactose-free milk
    - Snack: 3.5 oz. of skim yogurt
    - Lunch: 3/4 cup of Root Vegetable Soup
    - Snack: 3.5 oz. of Low Carb Green Smoothie
    - Dinner: 1 serving/ 1 cup of Pureed Classic Egg Salad
- **Tuesday**
    - Breakfast: ¼ cup of Egg whites
    - Snack: 3.5 oz. of skim lactose-free milk
    - Lunch: Garlic & Vegetable Soup
    - Snack: 3.5 oz. of skim yogurt
    - Dinner: Pumpkin Carrot Soup
- **Wednesday**
    - Breakfast: 3.5 oz. of skim lactose-free milk
    - Snack: 3.5 oz. of skim yogurt
    - Lunch: Creamy Carrot & Ginger Soup
    - Snack: Watermelon Strawberry Protein Smoothie
    - Dinner: Pureed Classic Egg Salad
- **Thursday**
    - Breakfast: 3.5 oz. of skim yogurt
    - Snack: 3.5 oz. of skim lactose-free milk
    - Lunch: Pineapple Coconut Smoothie
    - Snack: 3.5 oz. of skim yogurt
    - Dinner: Creamy Healthy Soup
- **Friday**
    - Breakfast: 3.5 oz. of skim yogurt
    - Snack: 3.5 oz. of skim lactose-free milk
    - Lunch: Strawberry Greek Yogurt Whip

- o Snack: Protein Hot Tea
- o Dinner: Mexican Egg Puree
- **Saturday**
  - o Breakfast: 3.5 oz. of skim yogurt
  - o Snack: 3.5 oz. of skim lactose-free milk
  - o Lunch: Light Tomato Soup
- **Snack:** Pineapple Coconut Smoothie
  - o Dinner: Chimichurri Chicken Puree
- **Sunday**
  - o Breakfast: 3.5 oz. of skim lactose-free milk
  - o Snack: 3.5 oz. of skim yogurt
  - o Lunch: Turkey Tacos with Refried Beans
  - o **Snack:** 3.5 oz. Diluted fresh squeeze sugar-free fruit juice
  - o Dinner: Creamy Carrot & Ginger Soup

Week 5

- **Monday**
  - o Breakfast: ¼ cup of Pureed fruits of your choice
  - o Snack: 3.5 oz. of skim yogurt
  - o Lunch: Mexican Egg Puree
  - o Snack: 3.5 oz. of skim lactose free milk
  - o Dinner: Chili Puree
- **Tuesday**
  - o Breakfast: 3.5 oz. Diluted fresh squeeze sugar-free fruit juice
  - o Snack: 3.5 oz. of skim yogurt
  - o Lunch: Lemon Garlic Pureed Salmon
  - o Snack: 3.5 oz. of skim lactose free milk
  - o Dinner: Light Tomato Soup
- **Wednesday**
  - o Breakfast: 3.5 oz. of skim lactose free milk
  - o Snack: 3.5 oz. Diluted fresh squeeze sugar-free fruit juice
  - o Lunch: Single Serve Baked Ricotta

- o Snack: 3.5 oz. of skim yogurt
- o Dinner: Chimichurri Chicken Puree
- **Thursday**
    - o Breakfast: 3.5 oz. Diluted fresh squeeze sugar-free fruit juice
    - o Lunch: No Chew Cheeseburgers
    - o Snack: Protein Hot Tea
    - o Dinner: Easy Egg Custard
- **Friday**
    - o Breakfast: 3.5 oz. of skim lactose free milk
    - o Lunch: Low-Fat Refried Beans
    - o Snack: fresh squeeze sugar-free fruit juice
    - o Dinner: Sweet Potato Puree
- **Saturday**
    - o Breakfast: 1 cup of skim milk
    - o Lunch: Chili Puree
    - o **Snack:** 3.5 oz. of skim yogurt
    - o Dinner: Buffalo Ranch Chicken
- **Sunday**
    - o Breakfast: Egg whites
    - o Snack: 3.5 oz. of skim yogurt
    - o Lunch: White Bean Soup
    - o **Snack:** fresh squeeze sugar-free fruit juice
    - o Dinner: Chicken & Black Bean Mole Puree

Week 6

- **Monday**
    - o Breakfast: Orange Tea
    - o Snack: skim yogurt
    - o Lunch: Chicken & Sweet Potato Puree
    - o Dinner: Rosemary Chicken with Blue Cheese
- **Tuesday**
    - o Breakfast: Skim Milk

- o Snack: Lemon Crystal Shake
- o Lunch: Mediterranean Chicken Puree
- o Dinner: Moroccan Fish Puree
- **Wednesday**
  - o Breakfast: Egg white
  - o Lunch: Ricotta & White Bean Puree
  - o Snack: Fruit juice
  - o Dinner: Pureed Vegetable
- **Thursday**
  - o Breakfast: Skim Yogurt
  - o Lunch: Green Protein Smoothie
  - o Snack: Orange Tea
  - o Dinner: Chicken & Sweet Potato Puree
- **Friday**
  - o Breakfast: Eggnog Protein Shake
  - o Snack: Skim Yogurt
  - o Lunch: Single Serve Baked Ricotta
  - o Snack: Fruit juice
  - o Dinner: Low-Fat Refried Beans
- **Saturday**
  - o Breakfast: Pumpkin Pie Protein Shake
  - o Lunch: Creamy Shrimp Scampi
  - o Snack: Skim yogurt
  - o Dinner: Red Pepper Enchilada Bean
- **Sunday**
  - o Breakfast: Pumpkin Pie Protein Shake
  - o Lunch: Turkey Tacos with Refried Beans
  - o Snack: Protein Hot tea
  - o Dinner: Creamy Shrimp Scampi

Stage 3: Week 7

You can follow the provided quantities (in the first week) for the rest of the meals in stage 3 or follow your dietitian's or doctor's advice. Do not forget to take your vitamins & supplements if given by the doctor. Dinner servings will be 1 serving from the recipe.

- **Monday**
    - Breakfast: 4.4 oz. skim milk with bread (2 slices)
    - Lunch: 0.7 oz. of Beef bone broth with grated cheese
    - Snack: One pureed apple of 5 oz.
    - Dinner: Turkey Meatloaf
- **Tuesday**
    - Breakfast: 4.4 oz. of low-fat Greek Yogurt with crackers
    - Lunch: Fat free Chicken broth
    - Snack: One pureed pear
    - Dinner: Lemon Garlic Pureed Salmon
- **Wednesday**
    - Breakfast: Skim milk with bread
    - Lunch: Zucchini Soup
    - Snack: Half bowl of pureed strawberries
    - Dinner: Buffalo Chicken Meatballs
- **Thursday**
    - Breakfast: Pumpkin Spice Hot Chocolate with crackers or bread slices
    - Lunch: Spinach Soup with Lemon
    - Snack: pureed fruit of your choice
    - Dinner: Turkey Kale Meatballs
- **Friday**
    - Breakfast: Shakshuka with bread slices
    - Lunch: Swede Soup
    - Snack: Fruit of your choice (pureed)
    - Dinner: Spicy Vegetarian Chili
- **Saturday**
    - Breakfast: Mocha Java with crackers
    - Lunch: Greek Yogurt Parfait
    - Snack: Berry Bomb

- o Dinner: Baked Fish with Almond Chutney
- **Sunday**
  - o Breakfast: Berry Avocado Smoothie
  - o Lunch: Power Chicken Salad
  - o Snack: One pureed apple
  - o Dinner: Chicken & Peanut Stew with crackers

Week 8

- **Monday**
  - o Breakfast: Chocolate Cherry Shake
  - o Lunch: Lentil, Haricot Bean & Chickpea Soup with crackers
  - o Snack: Non-fat Yogurt with strawberries
  - o Dinner: Lemon Garlic Salmon Baked
- **Tuesday**
  - o Breakfast: Cocoa Almond Protein Smoothie
  - o Lunch: Chicken Taco Chili
  - o Dinner: Italian Meatloaf
- **Wednesday**
  - o Breakfast: Skim milk with 2 slices of bread
  - o Lunch: Scotch Eggs
  - o Snack: Pumpkin Spice Hot Chocolate with crackers
  - o Dinner: Spicy Summer Beans & Sausage
- **Thursday**
  - o Breakfast: Pina Colada Protein Shake
  - o Lunch: Best High-Protein Soup
  - o Snack: One pureed fruit of your choice
  - o Dinner: Spicy Vegetarian Chili
- **Friday**
  - o Breakfast: Pina Colada Protein Shake
  - o Lunch: Soft Crab Salad with crackers
  - o Snack: Fruit of your choice
  - o Dinner: baked Fish with Almond Chutney

- **Saturday**
    - Breakfast: Ricotta Scrambled Eggs with bread
  - Lunch: Cranberry, Sage & Gruyere Turkey Meatballs
  - Snack: Sugar-free Tea with crackers
  - Dinner: Spinach & Feta Bake
- **Sunday**
  - Breakfast: **Berry Bomb**
  - Lunch: Chicken & Peanut Stew
  - Snack: Sugar-free Tea with crackers
  - Dinner: Chili Lime Turkey Burgers

Conclusion

Your gut processes the food you consume. After the bypass surgery, your stomach will be smaller. With less food, you will feel satisfied. Some sections of the stomach and small intestine that digest food will no longer absorb the food. As a result, the body will not receive all of the calories it needs from the food you consume. The surgeries may cause the stomach to shrink and a section of the intestine to be bypassed. Food is subsequently diverted to a section of the digestive system that is farther below. It goes around the tummy.

While all surgeries carry some risk, bariatric procedures done at recognized facilities are mostly risk-free. A team-based approach to bariatric surgery is required, with your surgeon, nutritionist, nurse, psychologist, and obesity medicine expert focusing on guiding you through each stage of the process. Patients who continue to eat healthily, exercise regularly, attend their appointments with obesity medicine specialists, and take vitamins and supplements as directed will fare better. Your bariatric care team will work with you for the rest of your life to help you achieve and maintain a lifelong healthy lifestyle, including dietary modifications and frequent physical exercise. Most patients need annual visits at their complete metabolic and bariatric surgery care facility, as well as frequent blood work testing to evaluate vitamin/ mineral levels.

If you're thinking of having gastric bypass surgery to help you lose weight, talk to your doctor first. The danger of consequences should be balanced against the risk of continuing to be obese. Keep in mind that gastric bypass surgery is most effective when coupled with a long-term, healthy lifestyle. Good nutritious eating habits and frequent exercise are two of them.

Made in United States
Orlando, FL
09 August 2022